The International Taxation
of Multinational Enterprises
in Developed Countries

THE INSTITUTE FOR
FISCAL STUDIES

The International Taxation of Multinational Enterprises in Developed Countries

J.D.R. ADAMS

J. WHALLEY

ASSOCIATED BUSINESS PROGRAMMES

LONDON

First published 1977

Copyright © I.F.S. 1977

All Rights Reserved. No part of this publication may be reproduced, stored in a retrieval system or transmitted in any form or by any means: electronic, electrostatic, magnetic tape, mechanical, photocopying, recording or otherwise, without permission in writing from the publishers.

Published by
Associated Business Programmes Ltd
17 Buckingham Gate London SW1

Produced by computer-controlled phototypesetting
using OCR input techniques by
UNWIN BROTHERS LIMITED
The Gresham Press, Old Woking, Surrey
A member of the Staples Printing Group
and printed offset by
A. Wheaton & Co., Exeter

ISBN O 85227 073 9

Contents

Preface

The interaction between multinational activity and domestic tax systems is a matter which in recent years has attracted increasing attention from both academics and public policy makers. We were approached some two years ago by the Institute for Fiscal Studies with a view to undertaking an enquiry of existing taxation arrangements towards multinational activity. Coming to this subject as generalists in our respective subjects we rapidly became aware of the need for an interdisciplinary approach to this topic.

In this monograph we seek primarily to provide a first source to which the general economist and lawyer might turn in order to acquaint himself with both the broad structure of present tax situations faced by multinational business in developed economies and rationalisations of various arrangements which might be pursued as alternatives. In this way we attempt to integrate the economic and legal aspects of the topic we address. The differences in approach of lawyers and economists show themselves in the different styles of chapters that are primarily legal or economic and we hope that readers will tolerate the slight discontinuities as a price of interdisciplinary effort.

Our limitation to developed economies is made solely on grounds of tractibility of the project, and our limited scope should not be construed as a view that the problems of less developed economies are either unimportant or uninteresting. We have also concentrated primarily on the structure of the legal arrangements and discussion of the principles at issue and have devoted only a minor portion of our study to administrative problems in this area. In particular, the issue of transfer pricing is one which is difficult to investigate fully in a study of this breadth and one on which, as the reader will see, we find it difficult to generalise as to the position in practice. Once again unimportance or lack of interest on our part should not be inferred.

We would also emphasise that we neither attempt to provide a tax compendium nor a practitioner's guide for use on a day to day or case by case basis.[1] We would hope, however, that we provide a source of material for use outside of the academic community although it is for clarification and stimulation of academic debate on these issues that we primarily write.

We wish to acknowledge the help and encouragement we have received from several quarters over a period of more than two years, while at the same time absolving all those named from any responsibility for the errors and omissions which inevitably remain. We are grateful to the Institute for Fiscal Studies for initiating and guiding this project, and in particular to Mrs Thelma Liesner for administering a most appropriate blend of encouragement and prompting for drafts. Mr J. Van Hoorn, Professor J.H. Dunning, and Professor C. Shoup have all read drafts at various stages and provided lengthy, informative, and corrective comments which have done the manuscript invaluable service. Mrs A. Smallwood of the Inland Revenue and Mr W.E. Pool, late of the Inland Revenue and more recently of the EEC, have both made extensive comments, provided much guidance, and have been the source of further enquiries. The International Committee of the Institute and in particular Mr J.F. Chown, Mr E. Nortcliffe, and Mr R.T. Pleasance have unstintingly given of their professional advice and corrected many errors.

1. We would refer the reader to the documentation produced by the International Bureau of Fiscal Documentation, Amsterdam, in the *European Taxation* and other series. A further reference is J.F. Chown *Taxation and Multinational Enterprise* Longman, 1974 which is much more a practitioner's guide.

1. Basic concepts and aims of the study

A Economic interdependence and multinational enterprises.

Economic relations between nations are increasingly being viewed in terms of economic interdependence. In this monograph we take up the issue of economic interdependence by examining taxation policy towards multinational enterprises at an international level.

In discussing interdependence of this form the distinction between the international movement of goods and services a. d the international movement of factors of production is fundamental. In the past international trade studies have focused primarily on the first of these issues. Recently, there has been an increasing tendency, reflected in this book, to consider policy towards international factor movements. We are thus concerned here with the international movement of capital, enterprise and know-how, and we attempt to analyse the role of international tax factors as they affect multinational enterprise in this process.

The object of our enquiry is the multinational as distinct from the domestic enterprise and below we clarify our understanding of this terminology. It is worth emphasizing that multinational activity represents direct foreign investment activity and is to be distinguished from the portfolio foreign investment which was more prevalent before the First World War.

The term 'multinational' refers to a particular form of conducting business on an international scale, but it is a word which has no legal (or for that matter taxation) status which distinguishes it as such; instead it has evolved through common usage, and must be used with some care. Broadly speaking, our interpretation of the term indicates a unified business operation organized into a corporate form which encompasses several countries.[1]

1.1 These multinational operations tend to be conducted through American, and to a less extent, British, Canadian, Japanese, or European parent

A multinational enterprise will centre on a company, usually predominantly located in one particular country, through which decision-making is undertaken for the whole of the enterprise's international operations. In many cases this company will control other companies operating in other countries through ownership of the voting stock of such companies (if not in total then by a majority holding). Where this method of organization is used we will term the controlling company the parent company and the controlled companies the subsidiary companies. We shall also refer to parent companies as operating in destination countries (the ultimate destination within the multinational enterprise of the profits of multinational activity); and subsidiary companies as operating in origin countries (the origin of the profits of multinational activity). In total the parent company, along with the connected subsidiary companies, will in these cases define the multinational enterprise.

In other cases, a multinational enterprise may operate not abroad through a subsidiary company, but instead undertake activity directly in the name of the parent company itself. Where the operation of a parent company extends in this way beyond a single country we term the operations of the parent company abroad as branch operations in origin countries. This distinction is important because the overall tax position of a parent/subsidiary operation may sometimes differ from that of a parent/branch operation.

The dividing line between what is and what is not a multinational enterprise is not as precise as is other terminology we shall use. There are a number of large domestic companies involved in activity abroad which is largely tangential to their primary operations which are purely domestic. The foreign operations of such companies will involve these organisations in the same taxation complications which are our concern here although the terminology 'multinational' is somewhat inappropriate for these enterprises.

We would also point out that even if a large proportion of the total activity of an enterprise is conducted in countries other than the destination country, the number of countries involved may be small. In such cases duonational or trinational enterprise might be a more appropriate term than 'multinational'. We use the term 'multi' to indicate more than one as the taxation position will typically be somewhat similar in broad outline for small numbered multi as well as large numbered multinational enterprises.

---

companies. In addition, there is a prevalent view that they operate abroad predominantly through subsidiary companies, although, as will be seen later, there is some ambiguity as to the precise position.

It should finally be stressed that we have limited ourselves to taxation policy towards multinational enterprises in developed countries. There are therefore multinational enterprises whose qualification for that title is activity primarily in less developed or developing countries. The taxation situation of these enterprises is not considered in this volume.

B Aims of the study

Our primary aim in this monograph is to outline the basic features of the tax treatment of multinational enterprises in developed countries and to present an evaluation of both present and alternative arrangements. As will become clear later, the technicalities of the tax position of most multinational enterprises are quite complicated as the operations of such activity come partly under the jurisdiction of one tax authority, and partly under others. Documentation of present arrangements in developed countries in complete detail is a task the size of which cannot be over-emphasized and our treatment is of necessity sparse in fineness of detail and coverage in some places.

Each country has special features of its tax treatment of domestic companies which are themselves of considerable importance. Documentation of these features, while tedious, is relatively simple compared to the complexities of the tax treatment of multinational enterprises which involves many pairs of countries. Multinational activity may also involve financial flows between third and even fourth countries along a route which leads ultimately to a parent company and the permutations on the network of possible countries can become very large indeed. Documenting all of these arrangements in their entirety must be beyond the scope of any single study and we can only hope to outline the major features of these arrangements in very general terms, illustrating particular examples where appropriate.

Where we turn to assessment of the impact of both present and alternative tax arrangements our task is equally difficult. Considerable disagreement exists among economists as to the appropriate model in which to consider the impact of domestic tax treatments of companies in isolation from an international setting.

Some authors are concerned with the shifting of corporate taxes through monopolistic power; others with a more general treatment of corporate taxes in a competitive context; others with the impact of corporate taxes on the financial structure of companies; and still others with the impact of corporate taxes on risk-taking. All of these views and more can be advanced when one turns to the far more complex world of multinational, as distinct from domestic, activity. In most of the cases we discuss we are only able to suggest the possible economic impact without being able to state which is empirically more accurate.

In the popular debate it is frequently suggested that multinational enterprises are able to obtain unfair tax advantages over other forms of enterprise. There is little firm empirical evidence on these matters and we would emphasize at this stage that we have not undertaken any detailed original research of an empirical nature in this study into these matters. We would go as far as to express doubt as to whether a question of this form can be given a meaningful interpretation when posed in such generality. These are, however, matters which attract much concern in the popular discussion of multinational activity, and we do attempt later to summarise some of the available material.[2] We have also attempted to analyse the view, at present gaining increasing support in some quarters, that no special recognition of the foreign tax liabilities of any business operation should be embodied in a nation's tax code. While we would regard such a view as simplistic, especially where a country is in a position of having both inward and outward investments, it is nevertheless a view which has attracted some attention and we attempt to give it a fair examination.

We would point out that although our concern is with multinational activity in developed countries, our scope for illustration has been more narrowly concentrated by necessity. We focus primarily on the present nine EEC countries, and (to a lesser extent) the United States, reaching out beyond only where an example of some interest is known to us. This, of course, does not mean to say that there are not many other examples of interest which we have not mentioned. Within our geographical area of specialization, we inevitably tend to return to British experience on many occasions as it is the system with which we are most familiar. We have tried to resist this temptation as much as possible, but this inevitably becomes our point of reference for the discussion of certain points.

It should finally be emphasized that our focus is the taxation of multinational enterprises and we only touch fleetingly on issues such as the special behaviour of these types of enterprises, reasons for their existence, and so on. These are matters dealt with extensively elsewhere.[3]

1.2 This material will be presented in more detail in the text, but for an example of one particular viewpoint on this matter the reader is referred at this stage to P.B. Musgrave *Tax Preferences to Foreign Investment* presented to the Joint Economic Committee of the US Congress, 11 June 1972.

1.3 See the excellent survey article by Dunning (J.H. Dunning 'The Determinants of International Production' *Oxford Economic Papers*, November 1973 pp. 289–337).

C   An outline of the taxation issues.

We would distinguish the tax treatment of multinational as against domestic enterprises by the fact that multinational enterprises typically come under the jurisdiction of more than one tax authority and the domestic tax treatment in each country typically differs. There is no clear presumption as to whether a multinational enterprise should enjoy the most favourable of the domestic tax treatments, the least favourable, some form of average, or a completely separate treatment. No clear prescription for a desirable set of arrangements for the total taxation of multinational enterprises exists.

Moreover, countries differ both with respect to the productivity of foreign investment received and their overall position as a net recipient or donor of foreign investment. There are therefore differing incentives for particular countries to tax multinational activity either harshly or leniently. One country may, for instance, have an incentive to tax inward investment harshly and outward investment lightly and another country the opposite incentive.

For these reasons, tax policies will tend to differ from country to country and as a result further (and complicating) incentives arise for countries to react to each others tax policies. The incentives for tax authorities in these matters are similar to the well recognised retaliatory features of tariff policy towards commodity flows between nations in contrast to the capital flows involved with multinational enterprises.

International agreements designed to mitigate the worst of these features exist;[4] but of course, agreements which are mutually beneficial and divide the gains from co-operation fairly are difficult to define, let alone achieve and maintain in a changing world. As we shall see, one of the results of the diversity of incentive is that tax treaties-exist on a bilateral rather than a multinational basis between nations, compounding[5] the complications inherent with the differing domestic legal structures.

As the tax treatment of multinational enterprises differs from that of domestic companies in coming under more than one tax authority, an

1.4 It is worth stressing that the position of multinational enterprises operating in particular countries (such as the US and in Switzerland) can become even more complicated due to the existence of state and local corporation tax liabilities. We have not taken up these complications in our study in any detail, although a comprehensive discussion of the position of a particular company cannot ignore their presence.

1.5 One can make the argument that the present system of nation states allows certain regions to pursue tax policies to attract foreign investment (such as Ireland) and that this diversity of tax structures eases regional problems which would be more severe under a harmonized single government regime.

understanding of the principles of domestic company tax systems is needed before the more complex multinational cases can be discussed. This we provide in the next and following chapters. We then move on to discuss the situation of multinational enterprises in the subsequent chapters.

2. An outline of the domestic tax treatment of companies

The international nature of the activities of multinational enterprises inevitably brings them within the scope of the tax provisions of several different countries. Double taxation arrangements exist between many countries of the world which alleviate this form of multiple tax liability. Before considering these arrangements, we provide a brief general description of the principal systems of domestic company taxation for readers who are unfamiliar with their main features. Those who are already familiar with these may prefer to omit both this and the following chapter.

A Introduction

1 Definition of company

The word company is used in this study to mean an entity which has under the law governing its creation an ownership of property and legal liability separate from the property and liability of its shareholders or other members. Thus under English law the property of ICI Ltd is not owned by the shareholders, but by the company itself. The property of the company will come into the ownership of the shareholders only to the extent that the company makes distributions, for example by way of dividends on the shares, or a transfer of the company's assets to the shareholders in the winding-up of a company being liquidated.

2 Suggested rationale of taxation of companies

Since a company's property is owned by the company and not by the shareholders it follows that income accruing to a company which is not distributed to the shareholders does not belong to them unless the company is wound up. Thus if taxes were levied on individuals only and not on companies, the undistributed profits of companies would escape taxation.

Some experts take the view that the levying of corporation taxes is justified simply on the ground that the company is a legal person separate from the persons who hold the shares in it or control it. The authors, however, take the view that this is not sufficient to justify a charge to tax on the company. Another explanation is that taxation of company profits is justified because otherwise profits accruing to companies would escape income taxation if they were not distributed to the shareholders. An alternative approach, however, is to tax the earnings per share of companies as income to the shareholders, whether distributed or not.

The authors' hypothesis is that, in the case of systems of taxation which do not treat undistributed profits as income of the shareholders, the taxation of companies on undistributed profits is justified on the grounds that otherwise an interest free loan of the ultimate income tax liability upon distribution is accorded the shareholders. It should, however, be noted that this justification is one for a relatively low rate tax on undistributed profits of companies and not for a higher rate tax on total company profits.

3 Meaning of profits

Different tax systems have different concepts of profit, but the expression 'profits' usually includes trading income and pure income.[1] Trading income is usually computed by taking gross receipts from the trade or business and subtracting such expenditure incurred in generating those receipts as the tax system concerned permits as a deduction in computing profits; generally only income and not capital expenditure is allowed as a deduction in computing trading income. Commonly, systems of tax give capital allowances which provide relief in respect of depreciation of specified types of capital assets.[2] Examples of pure income are: interest, royalties, income from portfolio investments owned by the company and dividends from subsidiary

2.1 The expression 'pure income' is used to denote receipts which are taxable without any deductions being allowed.
2.2 The tax relief in respect of capital allowances can take the following forms: a deduction in computing trading income, a deduction from trading income when it has been computed or a deduction from total profits.

companies. Under some systems of tax chargeable capital gains are included in the definition of company profits.[3]

4   Rate of Tax

Many systems provide for a flat rate of corporation tax, although they may also provide that companies with small profits and particular types of companies shall be taxed at lower rates.[4]

5   Taxation of distributions to shareholders who are individuals

Distributions to shareholders by way of dividends are subjected to personal income tax and some tax systems provide that on paying the dividend the company shall deduct tax at a stated rate and account to the revenue authorities for the tax so deducted.[5] If the payee's marginal rate of income tax is higher than the rate of tax withheld he will have to pay the extra; if his marginal tax rate is exactly the same as the rate of tax withheld then he will not be subjected to further tax on those payments, and if his marginal tax rate is lower than the rate of tax withheld he may be allowed a refund of the excess tax withheld.

The full impact of the tax system as it affects the income which shareholders receive can only be accurately assessed by considering both the tax on the company and the income tax on the shareholders.

6   Intercompany dividends

What is the corporation tax position where company A holds shares in company B and receives dividends from company B? Where the two companies are resident in different countries, the dividend may be subjected to tax in both countries and company A will have to rely on the

---

2.3 For example under the present UK system of corporation tax capital gains form part of the company's profits, but only a proportion of the gain is subjected to corporation tax.

2.4 Under the present UK system the normal rate of corporation tax is 52% for the financial year of 1975 (see the Finance Act 1976, section 25), companies whose profits do not exceed the prescribed limits are taxed at 42% (see the Finance Act 1972, Section 95 and the Finance Act 1974, section 10(2)), and industrial and provident societies, housing associations and building societies are taxed at 40% (see the Finance Act 1972, section 96, and the Finance Act 1974, section 10(3)). Hereafter Finance Acts will be denoted by the abbreviation FA. Lower rates of tax on small companies does occur in the American and Canadian systems of corporation taxation.

2.5 This was the case under the UK system which was in force from 1965–72; it is not the case, for instance, in the USA.

double taxation arrangements which exist in those two countries in order to alleviate this double tax burden.[6] If both companies are resident in the same country, then the companies will look to the domestic law in that country.

The policy underlying the UK tax legislation is that where profits accrue to a company resident in the UK and, out of those profits, that company pays a dividend which passes through one or more other UK resident shareholders, only one amount of corporation tax and only one amount of personal income tax shall be exacted. This result is achieved either by means of the group income provisions or by means of the franked investment income provisions.[7]

Some countries have a slightly different system which is as follows: company B's profits are subjected to corporation tax in the usual way. The dividend which company B pays is exempt from corporation tax in company A's hands, but the deductible expenditure allowed to company A is reduced by an amount equal to a prescribed proportion[8] of the dividend received from company B. The rationale of this is that the prescribed portion of company A's overhead expenses is deemed to have been expended in earning the company B dividend which is exempt from corporation tax and that portion of the overhead expenditure is therefore treated as non-deductible in the hands of company A.

7   Territorial scope

Generally countries will exact tax either if the taxpayer is resident in that country,[9] or if the source of the income or profit is situated in that country. Thus a company resident[10] in the UK is liable to UK corporation tax on its profits wherever arising[11] and a company resident

---

2.6 These arrangements will be discussed in subsequent chapters.

2.7 These will be explained below in section C of this chapter.

2.8 Under the French system the prescribed proportion is 5% of the gross dividend (including the imputation tax credit) which is 7.5% of the net dividend. This has the indirect effect of subjecting the dividend to corporation tax at 2.5% of the gross dividend (i.e. 3.75% of the net dividend).

2.9 The USA however, exacts tax on the grounds of US citizenship as well as residence.

2.10 Under the UK system a company is treated as residing where its central management and control actually abides, see *De Beers Consolidated Gold Mines v Howe* (1906) AC 455; *5 TC* 198 (HL). Cf. the USA system which uses the test of incorporation and not control.

2.11 Income and Corporation Taxes Act 1970, section 238 and 243(1). The abbreviation 'TA 1970' will hereafter be used to denote the Income and Corporation Taxes Act 1970.

abroad which carries on a trade through a branch or agency is liable to corporation tax on the profits of that branch.[12] A company distribution is taxable income under the UK system if the recipient (whether an individual[13] or a company) is resident in the UK[14] or if the dividend is paid on shares in a company resident in the UK.[15] Some systems of corporation tax treat branch income as a deemed distribution to the company and subject it to tax in the same way as a dividend paid by a subsidiary company to a parent company, but the UK system does not do this.

8 Closely controlled companies

A system of corporation tax may have special provisions to deal with companies which are under the control of a small number of shareholders. These are often small family companies where the members of the family are both shareholders and directors. The marginal rates of personal income tax of the shareholders may well be higher than the flat rate of corporation tax and therefore the shareholder-directors, who are in a position to determine whether dividends shall be paid, could in those circumstances secure a tax advantage by accumulating the profits in the company instead of distributing them. This advantage is usually nullified by provisions of the corporate tax code which deem a certain proportion of such a company's profits to have been distributed for the purpose of exacting personal income tax from the shareholders on such deemed distributions. The term 'close company' is used in the UK legislation to denote such a company.[16]

B Principal systems of corporation tax

There are three principal systems of corporation tax which operate in market economies, namely, the classical system, the imputation system

---

2.12 TA 1970, section 246(1) section 256(2) defines what branch profits are taxable.
2.13 Under the UK system it is a question of fact whether an individual is resident in the UK see: *Levene v IRC* (1928) AC 217; 13 *TC* 486 (HL), and *IRC v Lysaght* (1928) AC 234; 13 *TC* 511 (HL).
2.14 On the grounds that the taxpayer is situated in the UK.
2.15 On the grounds that the source is situated in the UK.
2.16 The definition of a close company is in the Income and Corporation Taxes Act 1970, section 282 and 283. It is very detailed and complicated but broadly, close companies are those which are controlled either by five or fewer shareholders or are controlled by shareholders who are directors.

and the two-rate system. These systems are distinguished by the way, if at all, they are integrated with the personal income tax system.

1   The classical system

Under this system profits accruing to a company are subjected to corporation tax, and distributions[17] to the shareholders are in addition subjected to personal income tax in their hands. Distributions to the shareholders are not deductible from the profits of the company for corporation tax purposes. Thus distributed profits are subjected both to corporation tax and personal income tax, whereas undistributed profits are subjected only to corporation tax. The total burden of tax borne by distributed profits is therefore higher than that borne by undistributed profits.

A justification which has been put forward for the classical system is that the company and the shareholders should each be subjected to a charge to tax because the company is a legal person separate from the shareholders and the total tax burden is justified on the ground that a number of small investors have obtained the advantage of being able to combine together to form a more powerful unit.[18] The authors do not subscribe to this point of view. Their opinion is that one should have regard to the total tax burden (including both corporation tax and personal income tax) and decide whether that burden is equitable and produces the desired economic effects. They do not take the view that it is justifiable to tax distributed profits at a higher rate than undistributed profits merely because the company is legally a separate person.

The UK adopted a classical system of corporation tax in 1965 with the express object of encouraging retention of profits by companies.[19] The desirability of such a system remains the subject of some debate and will be taken up later where the effects of the various systems of corporation tax are discussed.

We illustrate the operation of the classical system by means of the following examples:

Example 1. Where a tax code operates a classical system with a rate of corporation tax of 50% and a basic rate of personal income tax of 30%,

---

2.17 These will include profits of a small family company which are deemed to have been distributed.

2.18 Under the UK system of tax, a partnership could be used to obtain the advantage of combining to form a more powerful unit without suffering the severe tax burden imposed on distributed profits of companies.

2.19 See the Chancellor of the Exchequer's budget speech in 1965, Hansard 6 April 1965 Col 255.

the tax treatment of a profit of 100 accruing to a company would be as follows. If the profit were retained by the company, corporation tax of 50 would be charged on that profit.

If the profit were distributed by way of dividend to shareholders who were liable to the basic rate of personal income tax, but not to any higher rates of income tax the 100 would be treated as follows: The company would pay corporation tax of 50 on the 100; it would not be permitted to deduct the dividends in computing its profits for corporation tax purposes. The company would therefore be left with 50 to distribute by way of dividend. When that 50 was distributed to the shareholders by way of dividend, it would be subjected to basic rate personal income tax at 30% and therefore a further 15 would be paid in tax. Thus, if the company's profits were not distributed, they would be taxed at only 50%, whereas distributed profits would be subjected to tax of $50 + 15 = 65\%$.

One of the ways of avoiding this burdensome tax on distributed profits is for the company to raise capital by means of loans instead of shares. Interest payable on loans is normally deductible from the company's profits for corporation tax purposes with the result that the company does not pay any corporation tax on that slice of its profits which it uses to pay interest.

Example 2. Postulating the same rates of tax as in Example 1, the tax treatment of a profit of 100 used to pay interest to an individual, who had lent money to the company and who was liable to personal income tax at only the basic rate, would be as follows. The company would not pay any corporation tax on that 100, because the interest would be deductible in computing its profits for corporation tax purposes, and the recipient would pay personal income tax of 30. Thus the profit of 100 used to pay such interest would only suffer tax at 30%.

For this reason, the effect of the adoption of a classical system of corporation tax (and to a lesser extent the other systems discussed here) can be to cause companies to raise more capital by inviting loans (debt financing) and less by inviting the public to subscribe for shares (equity financing). To prevent too obvious tax avoidance, systems of corporation tax will often provide that payments of interest by companies at more than a commercial rate on loans to the company, or payments of interest on such loans at a rate which varies with the amount of the profits, are deemed to be dividends and are therefore taxable as distributions. These are provisions which deal with attempts to convert into debt finance for tax purposes, what for economic purposes is effectively equity finance.

2   *The imputation system*

Under the imputation system company profits are subjected to corporation tax as under the classical system, but, when the profits are distributed by way of dividend,[20] part of that corporation tax is treated as tax paid by the shareholder; i.e. part of the corporation tax is imputed to the shareholder as a credit against his liability to personal income tax on the distribution. The amount of the imputation obviously depends upon the policy of the government enacting the tax legislation.

Under the imputation system which has operated in the UK since 1 April 1973, the amount imputed to the shareholder is such as to give him a tax credit which exactly covers his liability to basic rate personal income tax. Thus the imputation system reduces the discrimination between the taxation of distributed and undistributed profits. Under the present UK system and under the system postulated in the next example, where profits are distributed to shareholders who are liable to personal income tax at only the basic rate, the total tax burden on those profits is the same as it would have been if the profits had not been distributed. We illustrate the operation of the imputation system by a further example:

Example 3. Where a tax code operates an imputation system with a rate of corporation tax of 50% and an imputation to the shareholders of 3/5ths of the corporation tax levied on the slice of profits distributed, and the basic rate of personal income tax is 30%, the tax treatment of a profit of 100 is as follows:

If the profit is retained the company would pay corporation tax of 50. If the profit is distributed by way of dividend to shareholders who are liable to personal income tax at only the basic rate the tax treatment of those profits would be as follows: The company would pay corporation tax of 50 and would be left with 50 available for distribution. The company can distribute that 50 to the shareholders without them having to pay any basic rate personal income tax, because the imputation covers this basic rate liability. Thus they receive 50 which is deemed to have been taxed at 30%. The gross amount of the dividend before tax was therefore 50 grossed-up. i.e.

$$\frac{50 \times 10}{7} = 71.43$$

They are theoretically liable to basic rate tax on that gross dividend of 71.43 at 30%, and therefore their national basic rate liability is 21.43.

2.20 This will include profits of a small family company which are deemed to have been distributed.

This basic rate liability is cancelled out by a tax credit which consists of imputing part of the corporation tax to them. The imputation is worked out as follows: it is 3/5ths of the corporation tax suffered by the company on that slice of its profits which is used to make the gross payment of the dividend. 50% of 71.43 = 35.72. 3/5ths of 35.72 = 21.43 which exactly covers the shareholders' basic rate liability on the gross amount of the dividend. Thus if the profit of 100 is distributed it will suffer total tax of 50% and if it is retained it will suffer the same amount of tax.

The tax treatment of a payment of interest to a person liable to tax at only the basic rate would be the same as in example 2, above.

Such an imputation system therefore removes the discrimination between the taxation of distributed and undistributed profits, in the case of shareholders who are liable to income tax at only the basic rate, but it only reduces and does not eliminate the difference between the amount of tax paid on profits used to pay dividends as compared with the tax levied on profits used to pay interest. Assuming that the recipient is only liable to basic rate tax in all cases, the postulated classical system taxes a dividend at 65% *in toto*, whereas interest is only taxed at 30%; the postulated imputation system taxes dividends at 50% and interest at 30%. Thus such an imputation system may still have to deem certain types of interest to be distributions to prevent tax avoidance.

3   The two-rate system

This system produces the same effect in domestic cases as the imputation system if corresponding rates are selected. It is in connection with negotiation of double tax arrangements that adopting an imputation rather than a two-rate system is thought by some to make a vital difference.[21] The example below produces the same effect in domestic cases as the imputation system postulated above. Under a two-rate system there is one rate of corporation tax applicable to undistributed profits and a lower rate applicable to distributed profits. The part of the profits used to pay the tax on the distributed profits is taxed as undistributed profit. The distributed profits are taxed at a lower rate to take account of the fact that they will also be subjected to personal income tax in the hands of the shareholders. Again it is possible to select rates which will result in the same total tax burden whether the profits are retained or whether they are distributed by way of dividend to shareholders liable to personal income tax at only the

---

2.21 This will be discussed in chapter 8, section C.

basic rate. We again illustrate the operation of the system by an example.

Example 4. Where a tax code operates a two-rate system of corporation tax, with a rate on undistributed profits of 50% and a rate of 20%[22] on distributed profits, and a basic rate of personal income tax of 30% the tax treatment of a profit of 100 accruing to a company would be as follows:

If the profit were retained by the company it would pay tax of 50. If the maximum amount of profit were distributed to basic rate shareholders, the company would pay corporation tax of 28.57. The 28.57 corporation tax is made up as follows: Corporation tax is charged at the lower rate of 20% on the gross distribution of 71.43. Corporation tax is charged at the higher rate of 50% on the sum of 28.57 used to pay the corporation tax. Thus the total corporation tax payable is:

$$71.43 \text{ at } 20\% = 14.29$$
$$28.57 \text{ at } 50\% = 14.28$$
$$\overline{ 28.57}$$

The remaining 71.43 distributed to the shareholders would be taxed at 30% = 21.43. Thus the total tax on the distributed profit would be 28.57 + 21.43 = 50%.

C   The systems of corporation tax which have operated in the UK over the last twenty years

The system of company taxation in the UK has been through a series of changes in the last twenty years, and each of the systems illustrates features of the systems discussed above. A closer examination of the UK arrangements will serve to illustrate in more detail features of a corporate tax system in operation and in addition will provide information which is relevant to the discussion of the overspill problem in chapter 11.

1   The pre-1965 system

Under this system company profits were subjected both to income tax at the standard rate and to an additional tax on company profits called

---

2.22   This rate has been selected so as to produce the same total tax burden as under the imputation system in example 3.

profits tax. Dividends were not deductible in computing profits for the purposes of either of those charges to tax. In 1963–64 the standard rate of income tax was 38.75% and the rate of profits tax was 15%; these rates will be used in the example which follows. When a company made a distribution out of profits which had been taxed in the company's hands at standard rate, the company was entitled to deduct and *retain* income tax thereon at the standard rate. Thus only one amount of standard rate tax was exacted whether the profits were distributed or not.

Example 5. A company resident in the UK had a profit of £100. On that it would pay income tax of £38.75 and profits tax of £15 making a total of £53.75, leaving £46.25 after tax. If the profit were distributed to shareholders resident in the UK the company would be able to declare a gross dividend of £75.51 from which it would be entitled to deduct tax at the standard rate of 38.75% and retain for itself the tax so deducted. Tax at the standard rate on £75.51 = £29.26 and therefore the net dividend payable would be £75.51 − £29.26 = £46.25. If the shareholders were only liable to standard rate income tax they would not be required to pay any further tax because the standard rate tax had already been deducted by the company at source. If a shareholder were liable to surtax the gross amount of the dividend (i.e. £75.51) would be included in his total income for surtax purposes, because surtax was an extra tax (at rates ranging from 10% to 50%) on top of the standard rate of income tax. If a shareholder were not liable to standard rate income tax (e.g. because he had sufficient unused personal reliefs) he could make a repayment claim.

Under this system company profits were taxed at the same rate whether they were retained or paid to shareholders liable to income tax at only the standard rate. The system was in effect, though not in legal form, an imputation system.

2   The system between 1965 and 1973

During this period the UK had a classical system with rates of corporation tax varying between 40% and 45% and a standard rate of income tax of 41.25% in some years and 38.75% in others. Thus in the year in which the rate of corporation tax was 45% and the standard rate of income tax was 41.25% the total burden on a company profit of £100 distributed by way of dividend to shareholders liable to standard rate income tax, but not to surtax, was £45 (corporation tax) + income tax at standard rate on the remaining £55 (= £22.69) = 67.69 per cent. The total burden on a profit of £100 distributed to a shareholder liable to the highest rate of surtax was: corporation tax of £45 + income tax of £22.69 + surtax of £27.5 = 95.19%.

3   Post–1973

From 1 April 1973 the UK has operated an imputation system of corporation tax. For the financial year 1973[23] the rate of corporation tax was 52%[24] and the basic rate of income tax for the year of assessment 1973–4[25] was 30%.[26]

a   Tax on company profits. Company profits[27] are subjected to corporation tax and profits are basically income profits computed according to income tax principles[28] and chargeable gains computed according to capital gains tax principles.[29] The chargeable gains of companies are reduced by 11/26ths and only the reduced gains are included in the company's profits liable to capital gains tax.[30] In computing trading income a company will be allowed to deduct income expenditure incurred for the purposes of the company's trade. Interest paid by a company will usually either be deductible as a trading expense in computing trading income[31] or will be deductible in computing the company's profits as a charge on income.[32] A company is permitted the same capital allowances as individuals.[33] Dividends are not deductible in computing company profits.[34]

Corporation tax is levied by reference to the company's own accounting periods, but the rates of corporation tax are fixed for each financial year (which runs from the beginning of April in one year to the

---

2.23 Which ran from 1 April 1973 to 31 March 1974.

2.24 See section 9 of the Finance Act 1974. There are the lower rates for companies with small profits and special types of companies, see section 10 and above at page 9 footnote 4.

2.25 Which ran from 6 April 1973 to 5 April 1974.

2.26 FA 1972, section 66. The basic rate for 1974–5 was 33%, for 1975–6 was 35% and for 1976–7 is 35% (see FA 1974, section 7, footnote No 2 Act 1975, section 25, and FA 1976 section 24).

2.27 As defined by TA 1970, section 238 (4).

2.28 TA 1970, section 249.

2.29 TA 1970, section 265.

2.30 FA 1972, section 93 (2) and the Finance Act 1974, section 10 (1) (a). A different fraction applies to authorised unit trusts.

2.31 Applying income tax principles.

2.32 Within the meaning of TA 1970, section 248.

2.33 See generally the Capital Allowances Act 1968 and particularly sections 73 and 74.

2.34 TA 1970, section 248 (2).

end of March in the next). If, as often happens, the company does not make up its annual accounts on 31 March so that the company's accounting periods straddle two financial years, the profits of the company in each accounting period are apportioned between the two financial years on a time basis and the rate for each financial year is applied to the slice of profit attributed to that financial year.[35] Suppose, for example, a UK resident company makes up its accounts each year on 31 December and in the accounting period which ended on 31 December 1974 it had trading profits of £100,000 and no capital profits. Three months of that accounting period fell in the financial year 1974 and nine months of that accounting period fell in the financial year 1975. Accordingly a quarter of those profits (£25,000) will be taxed at the rate of corporation tax in force in 1974[36] and three quarters (£75,000) at the rate in force in 1975.[37] The company will have to pay its corporation tax nine months after the end of its accounting period.[38]

b Taxation of distributions to individuals. Under the imputation system, when a company resident in the UK makes a qualifying distribution (which includes ordinary dividends paid out of income profits of the company),[39] the company must pay an amount of tax called advanced corporation tax[40] to the Revenue.[41]

This ACT serves two purposes: first, it represents a tax credit available to the recipient shareholders which will cover their liability to personal income tax at the basic rate,[42] and secondly the company can, subject to certain restrictions, set that ACT against its subsequent liability to corporation tax. The rate of ACT for the financial year 1973 was 3/7ths.[43] The two principal restrictions on the right of a company to set ACT against its liability to corporation tax are: first, ACT can only be set against the company's liability to corporation tax on its *income* profits[44] and, secondly, the set-off of ACT cannot be used to reduce the

---

2.35 See generally TA 1970, section 243.
2.36 Which is 52%.
2.37 Which is again 52%.
2.38 Assuming that the company commenced trading after 5 April 1965, see TA 1970 sections 243 and 244.
2.39 The definition of 'qualifying distribution' is in FA 1972, section 84 (4).
2.40 Hereafter denoted by the abbreviation 'ACT'.
2.41 FA 1972, section 84(1).
2.42 FA 1972, section 86.
2.43 FA 1972, section 84(2). The rate of ACT for 1974 was 33/67ths, for 1975 was 35/65ths and for 1976 is 35/65ths, (see FA 1974 section 12, F (No. 2) A 1975 section 28, and FA 1976 section 26).
2.44 FA 1972, section 85(2) and (6).

company's liability to corporation tax below a certain minimum amount.[45] Surplus ACT can be carried back and set against the company's corporation tax liability in any of its accounting periods beginning in the two previous financial years,[46] although it cannot be carried back and set against any liability to corporate tax charged for any time before 1 April 1973.[47] Any surplus ACT which is not dealt with by that means can be carried forward and used in future years.[48] Whether the surplus ACT is carried backwards or forwards, it cannot be set off in any accounting period so as to reduce the company's liability to corporation tax below that statutory minimum referred to above.

Example 6. X Ltd is a trading company resident in the UK but it is not a close company. X Ltd makes up its accounts each year on 31 March.[49] In the accounting period which began on 1 April 1973 and ended on 31 March 1974,[50] X Ltd had trading profits for corporation tax purposes amounting to £100,000. In February 1974, X Ltd paid a dividend totalling £35,000 to its shareholders, all of whom are individuals. On paying that dividend X Ltd will have been liable to pay to the Revenue ACT of 3/7ths of £35,000 = £15,000. X Ltd's liability to corporation tax will be 52% of £100,000 = £52,000 minus the ACT of £15,000 = £37,000.[51] Suppose that individual Y's share of that dividend was £35. The ACT constitutes a tax credit which covers his liability to basic rate.[52] Thus the gross amount of his dividend is £50. If Y is only liable to basic rate income tax he pays no more tax. If that dividend forms part of a band of his income taxed at 60%, he will have to pay tax on £50 = £30 minus the tax credit of 30% of £50 = £15, making a net liability to tax of £15. If he is not liable to tax on this dividend, for example because he has sufficient unused personal reliefs, he will be able to recover the £15 tax credit.

The minimum corporation tax liability is arrived at by applying

---

2.45 See FA 1972, section 85(2). For the financial year 1973 this minimum was 22%.
2.46 FA 1972, section 85(3).
2.47 FA 1972, section 85(7), that is because the imputation system did not come into operation until 1 April 1973.
2.48 FA 1972, section 85(4).
2.49 For the sake of simplicity the example postulates that the company's accounting periods coincide with the financial year.
2.50 This example and the subsequent examples in this section are set in the financial year 1973 because the rates of taxes for those years produce the simplest figures.
2.51 This figure is above the statutory minimum corporation tax liability, see footnote 2.45 above.
2.52 FA 1972, section 86. The basic rate for 1973–4 was 30%.

Finance Act 1972 section 85(2) which provides that a company cannot set off against its liability to corporation tax in any given accounting period more than a prescribed amount of ACT. This maximum amount of ACT which can be set off in any given accounting period is, in the words of the statute, 'ACT on a distribution which together with the ACT payable in respect of it is equal to the company's income chargeable to corporation tax for that period'.[53] What this means is that one has to calculate what would be the maximum dividend which the company could pay out of its income profits on the assumption that only ACT was chargeable and not corporation tax. The maximum amount of ACT which can be set off in the accounting period concerned is ACT on that hypothetical dividend.

Example 7. Take the same facts as example 6 except that X Ltd paid a dividend of £140,000 in February 1974.[54] When paying that dividend X Ltd would have to pay ACT of £60,000 to the Revenue. Not all that ACT could be set against X Ltd's liability to corporation tax on its income profits of £100,000 in that year. One takes the income profits of £100,000 and calculates what is the maximum distribution the company could have made if it only had to pay ACT. The answer is £70,000 because the ACT on a distribution of £70,000 would be £30,000 and thus a distribution of £70,000 plus the ACT on it would consume the whole £100,000. ACT on that hypothetical distribution of £70,000 is £30,000 and therefore the maximum amount of ACT which X Ltd can set against its corporation tax liability for the accounting period ended on 31 March 1974 is £30,000. Thus its corporation tax liability for that period is £52,000 minus ACT of £30,000 which makes £22,000. In this case the surplus ACT cannot be carried backwards because that would take it back before 1 April 1973, therefore it can only be carried forwards.

c Inter-company dividends. What is the position where one UK resident company receives a dividend from another UK resident company?

Where the group income provisions apply,[55] the following rules operate. Both companies can jointly elect that the company paying the

---

2.53 FA 1972, section 85(2).
2.54 The company could pay a dividend of this amount either because it had accumulated profits from earlier years, or because it had realised capital profits in that year. ACT cannot be set against corporation tax on capital profits.
2.55 TA 1970, section 256(1) defines group income. The group income provisions will apply, for example, where the company paying the dividend is a 51%-plus subsidiary of the company receiving them.

dividend can pay it without liability to ACT.[56] The company receiving the dividend will then have to pay ACT if it uses that dividend to make a distribution outside the group. The company receiving the dividend will not pay any corporation tax on that dividend.[57]

Example 8. Company B is a 100% subsidiary of company A and therefore the group income provisions apply.[46] Company B pays a dividend to company A of £50,000 out of income profits. Company B need not pay any ACT if both companies elect to apply the group income provisions. Company A pays no corporation tax on that £50,000. If company A decides to distribute that £50,000 to its shareholders it will be able to pay £35,000 to the shareholders by way of dividend and will have to pay ACT of £15,000 thereon.

Where the group income provisions do not govern the case, either because they do not apply or because the companies have decided not to invoke them, the franked investment income provisions will apply instead. Under the franked investment income provisions, the company paying the dividend will have to pay ACT on it. The company receiving it will not pay any corporation tax on that dividend and the dividend will constitute franked investment income in the hands of that company.[58] Subject to very limited exceptions the company receiving the dividend cannot obtain a refund of the ACT paid by the company which paid the dividend, but that ACT can be used to frank the recipient company's liability to ACT on its own distributions with the result that the recipient company will only be liable to pay ACT on its own distributions to the extent that they exceed its franked investment income.[59] The individual shareholders of the company which received the franked investment income will be entitled to a tax credit in respect of the dividends they have received from that company in the usual way.[60]

Example 9. Company A owns shares in company B but the companies do not form part of a group. Company B pays a dividend of 65 to company A. Company B will be liable to pay ACT in respect of that dividend. Company A will not be liable to corporation tax on the dividend it has received from company B. Company A then pays a dividend of 65 to the individuals who own its shares. Company A will not be liable to pay ACT on that dividend of 65 which it has paid to its

---

2.56 TA 1970, section 256(1).
2.57 TA 1970, section 239.
2.58 FA 1972, section 88.
2.59 FA 1972, section 89.
2.60 FA 1972, section 86.

shareholders because its distributions do not exceed its franked investment income. The shareholders in company A will be entitled to a tax credit of 35 in respect of the dividend they have received.

Thus the effect of both the group income provisions and the franked investment income provisions is that only one amount of ACT is payable on the income flow, and the individual shareholders are given a tax credit to cover their basic rate liability in just the same way as if the dividend had been paid without passing through company A. The result is the same no matter how many UK resident companies the income passes through on its way to the individual UK shareholders.

d Losses and group relief. Companies are given relief in respect of losses in the same way as individuals.[61] Where the companies form a 'group' for 'group relief' purposes[62] then the reliefs known as group relief are available to the companies; these are principally the right of one company in the group to pass losses and capital allowances to another company, so that the recipient company obtains the tax relief in respect of them.

e Close companies. The income of close companies[63] can be apportioned to the shareholders for the purpose of exacting personal income tax from them at the higher rates and the additional rate on investment income, if the company fails to make distributions up to the required standard. The required standard is 100% in the case of investment income and in the case of trading income is 50%, or such less amount as is justified to the inspector on the grounds of the requirements of the company's business.[64] A company is not a close company if it is controlled by another company which is not a close company. Thus if company A, which is not a close company, controls company B, company B is not a close company either.[65]

2.61 TA 1970, section 177–9.
2.62 TA 1970, section 258. NB the definition of a group is different from the definition for the purposes of the group income provisions.
2.63 As defined in TA 1970, sections 282 and 283.
2.64 FA 1972, section 94 and schedule 16.
2.65 Even though it is controlled by one person. This is because it is specifically exempted from the definition of a close company by TA 1970, section 282(4).

Appendix to Chapter 2

Table of corporation tax systems in the EEC[1] countries other than the UK[2]

Country	Type of system	Main features
Belgium	Imputation	Corporation tax of 42% (with lower rates for companies with small profits).
		Witholding tax on dividends of 20% of the gross dividend.
		The tax credit given to an individual shareholder is 45% of the net dividend.
		Profits of a branch are taxed at 48% but there is no withholding tax on payments by the branch to the parent.
Netherlands	Classical	Corporation tax of 48%
		Withholding tax on dividends of 25% of the gross amount of the dividend.
		Profits of a branch are subject to corporation tax, but there is no withholding tax on payments by that branch to the parent.
France	Imputation	Corporation tax of 50%
		There is no withholding tax on dividends paid to residents of France, but dividends paid to non-residents are subjected to a withholding tax of 25%.
		The shareholders are given a tax credit (called *avoir fiscal*) of 50% of the dividend received.
		The profits of a French branch of a foreign resident company are subjected to the normal rate of corporation tax and the balance is liable to withholding tax as if it were a dividend.
West Germany	Two-rate	Corporation tax of 51% on undistributed profits and 15% on distributed profits. Because the part of the profit which is used to pay the tax on the distribution is taxed at 51% as an undistributed profit, the effective rate on distributed profits is 23.4%. At present these rates are subject to a 3% surcharge giving a rate of 52.33% on undistributed profits and an effective rate of 24.55% on distributed profits.
		There is a dividend withholding tax at 25%
		A German branch of a foreign resident

---

1 There is a description of the US corporate tax system in chapter 10.

Country	Type of system	Main features
		company is liable to corporation tax at 49%, but there is no withholding tax on payments by the branch to the company. It has been proposed that the German system should be changed to one which is a mixture of the two-rate and the imputation systems, involving a higher rate than 15% on distributed profits and part of this will be imputed to the shareholders as a tax credit.
Denmark	Classical	Corporation tax rate of 37%. There is a withholding tax of 30% on dividends. Profits of a Danish branch of a foreign resident company are taxed at 34% (without any deduction) but payments by the branch to the company are not subjected to withholding tax.
Luxembourg	Classical	Corporation tax rate of 40%. There is a withholding tax on dividends of 15%. The profits of a Luxembourg branch of a foreign resident company are subject to the normal rate of corporation tax, but there is no withholding tax on payments by the branch to the company.
Eire	Imputation	Income tax at 35% + corporation profits tax of 23%. The corporation profits tax is deductible from the profit on which income tax is charged, thus producing an effective rate on company profits of 49.95%. No withholding tax on dividends. The dividend is regarded in the shareholders' hands as a net dividend which has suffered income tax at 35% (i.e. the shareholder is given a tax credit of 35% of the grossed-up dividend).
Italy	Classical	The basic rate of corporation tax is 25% plus additional charges which take the average rate for most corporations into the range 35-40%.

2 For a detailed exposition of the tax systems see *Guides to European Taxation* published by the International Bureau of Fiscal Documentation in Amsterdam (particularly volumes II and III).

3. The economic impact of domestic company taxation

In chapter 2 we have outlined the broad structure of domestic systems of company taxation drawing particular attention to three types of corporation tax system in use in various economies; the classical, two rate, and imputation systems. We suggested that some appreciation of the structure of domestic arrangements is necessary before a grasp of the tax position facing multinational enterprises can be obtained.

In similar vein we go on in this chapter to consider various economic theories which have been presented of the impact on the economy of domestic company taxation arrangements. As with the explanation of tax arrangements, it seems natural to consider the behavioural speculations of economists on the impact of company taxation when limited to purely domestic situations before moving on to the more complex world of multinational activity. As will be seen, a number of different viewpoints of the simpler domestic situation have been presented, and economists have by and large restricted themselves to attempting to resolve the various arguments for this case. As a result little attention has been paid by economists to the more complex situations involving enterprises trading across national boundaries, and in later chapters we attempt to draw what lessons we can from the domestic cases for assessments of the impact of taxation on multinational enterprises.

In this chapter we take up four of the main strands within the economics literature on the impact of company taxation; the issue of the so-called 'shifting' of the corporation tax; the general equilibrium viewpoint of the matter; the interrelation of corporation tax and corporate financial policy; and the effects of corporation tax on risk-taking.

A 'Shifting' of company taxation

The issue of 'shifting' of company taxation is one that in recent years has attracted a considerable amount of attention from economists. While it is the company that discharges the legal tax liability that is placed upon it, a number of economists have suggested that companies will alter their behaviour as tax liabilities change so that the increased burden of tax resulting from a tax increase is transmitted (shifted) to other economic agents. A distinction is sometimes drawn between 'forward shifting' and 'backward shifting' of the tax. Forward shifting would be represented by an increase in product prices in response to a tax increase, the tax being partly (or wholly) shifted forward on to consumers of the product via increased prices. Backward shifting would be represented by a decrease in wages paid to workers in response to a tax increase, the tax being partly (or wholly) shifted backward on to suppliers of productive inputs via the remuneration paid to them by the firm.

The issue of shifting is of considerable consequence from a distributional point of view. If company taxation is to be justified (as it often is) as an attempt to remedy an imbalance within the tax system in favour of stockholders, then a tax shifted on to someone else may be at best ineffective and at worst counter-productive.[1] A distinction between long run and short run adjustment within the economy should be kept in mind when discussing this issue. Long run adjustments within the economy in response to a change in company taxation arrangements will inevitably involve price changes as the pressures of competition force firms to leave industries made unprofitable by tax changes, and enter those now made relatively attractive. This long run pattern of adjustment is not the primary point at issue in the shifting argument as there is a reasonable consensus that in the long run some degree of shifting will take place. The focus of the shifting discussion is more on short run adjustment.

The position of classical economists on such a matter would be that in the short run firms are competitive price taking agents. Attempts by individual firms to increase prices would result in zero sales of outputs and attempts by similar firms to cut factor costs would place them in the position of being unable to hire the services of productive inputs. It is

---

3.1 It is interesting to note that those economists who have claimed empirical findings that the tax is shifted forward have not gone on to argue for the removal of corporation tax, although this would seem the natural prescription from such a finding.

this position which in recent years has come into question in the shifting debate as economists have sought to take into account the oligopolistic character of many industries.

One of the best known of positions taken by economists in the shifting discussion in connection with the impact of corporation tax is that of Kryzaniak and Musgrave.[2] They suggest a model of the economy characterized by producers with considerable market power (a monopoly or oligopolistic element) which differs from industry to industry. In Kryzaniak and Musgrave's view it is the extent of this power that determines the degree to which the corporation tax is shifted forward from producers on to consumers.[3] Corporation taxation is seen as an attempt to tax company profits. If producers are able in the short term to alter their output pricing[4] and quantity decisions in response to changes in corporate tax rates in such a way as to preserve net of tax corporate profits as tax rates change, then the tax is, in the Kryzaniak-Musgrave terminology, said to be shifted forward by producers on to consumers. A complete shifting as described here is termed 100% shifting, but, of course, intermediate degrees of shifting down to 0% are possible depending upon the extent of market power. Thus, for Kryzaniak and Musgrave the important question concerning corporate taxes is the degree of shifting which, in turn, determines the incidence of the tax; whether it falls on profits or on consumers. 100% shifting corresponds to a situation where producers use their market power to adjust output prices as corporation tax rates change, so as to exactly preserve the net of tax rate of return on employed capital.

Using US data for the period 1935–44 and 1948–59 Kryzaniak and Musgrave have attempted to estimate the effect on the before tax rate of return on capital in US manufacturing industry of changes in the corporate tax liability which have resulted from changes in the corporate tax rate in the US. They have found an elasticity of the gross of tax return on capital with respect to the tax liability parameter of greater than 1.0, which implies there is more than 100% shifting of corporate taxes (increases in corporate taxes actually increase the after tax return).

This result has always seemed somewhat implausible to a number of economists, and Kryzaniak and Musgrave's work has been the subject

---

3.2 M. Kryzaniak and R.A. Musgrave 'The Shifting of the Corporation Income Tax' 1964.
3.3 Kryzaniak and Musgrave do not consider the possibility of backward shifting.
3.4 This, of course, finesses problems presented by price controls which currently operate in the UK.

of considerable discussion and some criticism. The specification of the particular empirical estimation procedures they use has been queried and the justification for the non-tax variables included in their calculations discussed. The sample period chosen in their study has also been criticised. As there were low corporate tax rates during the US depression (the first of Kryzaniak and Musgrave's sub-periods) and high corporate tax rates after the war (a period of expansion), to some extent their results merely reflect the similar movement over time of unemployment and profits.[5] Some researchers have added other variables to the specification adopted by Kryzaniak and Musgrave, and adjusted the time period; this has changed the degree of shifting from up to 130% for particular industries down to 60%.

More substantive criticisms have been made by Gordon[6] and Turek.[7] Using a model with a constant rate of profit mark up, and examining data on various industries Gordon finds degrees of shifting which markedly depend on degrees of concentration within industries. For chemicals, and rubber production in the US he finds 90% shifting of the corporate tax whereas for food a figure close to zero is obtained, for textiles a negative shifting is found. Overall for all of US manufacturing industry Gordon produces a figure which is much lower than the figures obtained by Kryzaniak and Musgrave (around 20%).

Turek has been concerned to take account of the effects of the corporation tax as it causes adjustments in the capital-labour ratios of companies in their production processes. This requires an explicit production function model and constant elasticity of substitution functions are used. Turek, however, finds an even lower degree of shifting overall than Gordon (some 12%) but emphasises the wide margin of error around this figure.

In economies other than the USA there has as yet only been a limited amount of investigation of the shifting question. It is, however, worth emphasizing the suggestion made by Prest[8] that the more open is the

---

3.5 As Shoup has pointed out, it is also the case that the findings of Kryzaniak and Musgrave include the effect of the increase in government expenditures that the rise in the corporate tax rate financed over this period. This income effect of government expenditures in the corporate sector may have been powerful enough to (at least partially) maintain the net of tax rate of return on employed capital. (See C.S. Shoup *Quantitative Research in Taxation and Government Expenditures* NBER. Columbia University Press 1972 pp. 19–20).

3.6 R.Gordon 'The Incidence of the Corporation Income Tax' *American Economic Review* September 1967.

3.7 J.Turek 'Short-run shifting of the Corporate income tax' *Yale Economic Essays* Spring 1970.

3.8 A.R. Prest *Public Finance* (5th Edition, 1975) p. 362.

economy (and hence the more export oriented) the more restricted will be the opportunities to pass on tax increases via price increases. This is a view that seems to be supported for the UK by the limited amount of empirical evidence that is available.[9]

Overall there is some disagreement among academic economists on the importance of shifting of the corporation tax (in the sense which Kryzaniak and Musgrave present their analysis) within domestic economies. These notions of shifting of corporation taxes, however, will become important in our later discussions of the tax treatment of multinational activity. Such enterprises typically have considerable power in the market place through patent and royalty rights or high shares[10] of particular markets, and thus casual observation might suggest that the ability of multinational enterprises to shift the corporate tax forward on to consumers may well exceed that of domestic companies. This last point has the important implication that a host country may well be reluctant to tax a subsidiary company of a foreign parent if that tax is more than passed on to domestic consumers in the host country. If, however, little shifting occurs in these cases the government of a host country in which a multinational subsidiary company is located will not be too concerned about the results of high tax rates that it might place on the multinational operation if the tax is all shifted on to the shareholders of the parent company who are predominantly located in the foreign country. As we shall see later this latter argument can be used as a nationally based economic justification for harsher taxation of multinational enterprises operating within national boundaries than of purely domestic companies.

B   The general equilibrium view of company taxation.

A completely different approach to the economic impact of company taxation to that represented by the literature on the shifting of the tax is revealed in the general equilibrium approach to assessing the impact of corporation taxation. This line of approach has been particularly explored by Harberger in a series of articles.[11] Harberger sees

3.9 J.M. Davis 'An Aggregate Time Series Analysis of the Short-Run Shifting of the UK Company Tax' *Oxford Economic Papers*, July 1972.

3.10 These high shares are often themselves a reflection of the power generated through the use of trademarks and other methods of brand identification.

3.11 A.C. Harberger 'The incidence of the corporation income tax', *Journal of Political Economy 1962*; A.C. Harberger 'Efficiency effects of taxation of income from capital' in M. Kryzaniak (ed). *Effects of corporation tax* (1966).

corporation taxation as a principal component of an entire system of taxation of income from capital which is 'discriminatory' across industries. The profitability of investments made in the various alternative uses for capital (investments) is one of the central features of the general equilibrium approach. This view suggests that although the net of tax price of capital services may be equalized in its alternative uses by market forces, the gross of tax prices will be made unequal by taxation. The gross of tax price represents the value to society of the increment of output produced by employment of a marginal unit of capital services, and hence from a social point of view, too much capital tends to be employed in relatively lightly taxed industries, and too little in highly taxed industries.

Unlike the shifting discussion which is motivated by a concern with distribution, the general equilibrium approach is motivated more heavily by efficiency considerations. That is, how company taxation via artificial incentives results in society making an inefficient use of the resources available to it. By reform of the system of company taxation, it is argued, society as a whole can achieve a gain in real income which is quite separate from the way in which total income is distributed.

It is important, however, to stress that this approach considers not only corporation taxes but all taxes which Harberger considers to 'fall' on income as a return to capital. Besides corporation tax other components of the tax system such as personal income taxes, capital gains taxes (if any), and property taxes (rates in the UK) are included in Harberger's view of the impact of taxation of income accruing to capital.[12]

The operation of an entire system of taxation of income as a return to capital is thus viewed by Harberger as distortionary in the sense that different industries face different effective[13] tax rates which cause society to make an inappropriate use of resources. It should be pointed out that these industry wide differentials in effective tax rates are not a

---

3.12 It is worth bearing in mind that the general equilibrium approach works in terms of what economists term 'effective' tax rates (as against 'legal' tax rates). By this is meant that from a behavioural point of view the tax payment and/or basis for determining tax liability differ from the view manifest in law. Thus the economist may aggregate two or more legal taxes into one effective tax on an income flow by treating both company and individual taxation as one single effective tax on the flow of profit income made via a company to a shareholder. Alternatively, the economist may redefine the tax base from its legal definition to capture more realistically behavioural characteristics. An example of this last point is the preference of large numbers of economists to include capital gains (on an accrual basis) in personal income even though this is not done in the income tax system.

3.13 See footnote 12.

reflection of specific industry taxes or subsidies which are defined by law. The differentials instead result from a number of features in the administration and operation of the whole of the capital income tax system of which company tax is but a part. Thus in the general equilibrium approach the integration of company tax with the whole of the tax system is heavily stressed in evaluating its impact on the economy.

The features of the capital income tax system that cause differential effective capital income tax rates to operate across industries may be outlined as follows:

1 Corporation tax is payable only if an enterprise is incorporated. Those industries organized heavily on an unincorporated basis (such as agriculture and real estate in the USA, and to a lesser extent construction and professional services in the UK) tend to face lower effective tax rates. This is a feature emphasized strongly by Harberger.[14]

2 Capital gains realized by individuals are typically[15] taxed at rates lower than other personal income and, importantly, on a realisation rather than on an accrual basis. Especially under a classical corporation tax system, corporate profits which are paid to stock holders via the company retaining profits, investing the funds, and converting[16] the

---

3.14 This situation is in practice not quite as simple as suggested above. To some extent individuals can take profits out of companies they control through directors fees which are deductible from the corporate profits tax base. Equally, individuals taking capital income through a company which retains large proportions of profits and pays them out via capital gains may be better off than if organized in partnership or proprietorship form due to the income tax treatment of capital gains even though company tax would not be avoided. This last point, in the UK context, inevitably becomes involved with the close company provisions.

3.15 This is the situation, for instance, in the US and the UK. In a number of European economies, such as Italy and France, capital gains are effectively not taxed at all except for a limited number of cases.

3.16 Economists are prone to think in terms of simple mechanistic transformation of retained profits into an increased stock market price for the equity of the company that represents the net worth acquired by way of cash via retention. In practice, of course, things are a good deal more complicated than this. There is evidence, albeit limited, to suggest that the equity valuation of companies and their net worth in terms of asset values minus liabilities do not coincide. (See, for instance, J. Revell *The Wealth of the Nation* Cambridge University Press, p. 60) This is a source of some puzzlement to economists (who sometimes react by suggesting the evidence is wrong) as a lower equity value would give incentive for stockholders to sell all the assets, and a higher equity value incentive for the company to sell equity and buy assets. To the

original profit into a capital gain for the company shareholders, typically will attract a lower rate of total taxation by this means than if paid out directly via a dividend. While the same payment of corporation tax will be made under a classical corporation tax system whether profits are retained or distributed, the payment of income (or capital gains) tax by the stockholder will be very much dependent upon the retention/distribution decision. In practice, various industries tend to have different dividend to payout ratios, and thus these industries tend to face lower total effective tax rates (corporate taxes plus personal income taxes or capital gains tax paid by the recipient shareholder) on capital income paid to stockholders.

Under an imputation or two-rate corporation tax system the incentive for companies to retain profits is less powerful and the incentive may actually work in favour of distribution. Where, as in the UK, the credit is such that a significant number of income taxpayers would pay no further personal income tax on receiving a distribution in the way of a dividend, those stockholders in or below the basic rate income tax brackets, would in effect pay increased total taxes if a company adopted a retention policy.

An overall result of this treatment of capital gains is that, depending somewhat on the system of corporation tax in use, one can expect to find companies with different financial policies associated with different groups of stockholders (particularly under a classical corporation tax system); low payout high retention companies with high income stockholders; and high payout low retention companies with low income stockholders. In the general equilibrium approach it is, however, the industry wide differences in retention policy which are emphasized as producing different effective total tax rates across industries.

3 Interest payments made to service the debt of a company are deductible from trading profits in determining the corporation tax base. Interest payments are, in fact, broadly treated in this way as a deductible business cost under all corporate tax systems in industralised nations, but, many economists argue for the inclusion of such payments as part of the total income return to capital which accrues to all claimants on companies which operate in the economy. Under this view, interest

---

extent that this is true conversion of increased assets into higher stock prices may be far from automatic. Furthermore, highly specialized firms may well be in the position of experiencing diminishing returns to incremental investments, and so increased net worth via acquisition of more capital equipment may yield a less than proportional increase in stock market price.

payments represent a way in which the income of the corporate sector can be paid to claimants in the personal sector without corporation tax being paid. For individuals receiving income from a company the total tax liability incurred will tend to be reduced[17] if the company adopts debt financing instead of equity financing. Thus, those industries having higher than average debt to equity ratios will also tend to face lower effective tax rates in total on this broadly defined notion of income accruing to capital employed in various industries.

4 Allowances for depreciation of capital assets are granted under many corporation tax systems which often show considerable acceleration relative to 'true' depreciation (the UK now has 100% first year allowances on plant and machinery).[18] As different industries typically employ capital assets with differing actual service life streams this acceleration in the depreciation allowances can be thought of as giving an interest-free loan of differing size to different industries. Thus a further differentiation in the effective total tax rates on income as a return to capital in various industries is introduced.

All of these features outlined above produce a system of taxation of income from capital which produces differential total tax rates in the different industries of the economy. Company taxation is a major element in this system. Harberger's view is that this situation results in an inefficient allocation of resources as over employment of capital services in lightly taxed (principally unincorporated) industries is encouraged.

In addition to locating this source of inefficiency one can also attempt to calculate the gain which would accrue to the economy from the abolition of the distortionary features of the system of taxation of income from capital. This has been attempted by Harberger in the context of a simple two sector (high and low tax industries), two factor of production, general equilibrium model of the US economy for the period 1953–9. The distortionary features of the system of taxation of income from capital can be removed in this model and the behaviour of the economy simulated under competitive assumptions. It is found that the gain to the economy from removal of the distortionary features of

---

3.17 This feature is in fact somewhat complicated and is inter-linked with feature 2. Equity financing involves a company tax liability but gives the opportunity for a retention policy which may be so advantageous for high income individuals that it outweighs the saving in corporate tax liability.
3.18 Some countries, e.g. Denmark, give some deduction in advance of investments. A limited amount of corporation tax liability can be set aside provided the funds saved are used for investment purposes within a specified number of years.

this tax system is some 1.5% – 1% of GNP.[19] The conjecture is offered that a large part of this gain would be realized by a removal of corporation tax in the US and other economies.

Although not a major concern of the general equilibrium approach the question of the shifting of corporation tax can also be analyzed in this framework. In contrast with the findings of Kryzaniak and Musgrave, the burden of the tax is found to lie primarily on the recipients of capital income (the shareholders). This conflicts with the view of Kryzaniak and Musgrave that the corporate tax is shifted to consumers from producers. While it is true that this model produces results markedly different from those of Kryzaniak and Musgrave, Harberger's view has also been found deficient by some authors primarily because it ignores the role of corporate financial policy in the determination of corporate tax liability. This is the issue to which we turn next.

C   Corporate taxes and corporate financial policy

In previous two sub-sections we have explored two views of the economic effects of corporate taxes on the operation of domestic economies. The Kryzaniak-Musgrave (shifting) argument is concerned with the extent to which corporations bear the burden of corporate taxes via a reduction of profit margins, and the extent to which the corporation tax is shifted forward on to consumers or back to wage earners and lenders. The Harberger (general equilibrium) discussion views the corporate tax as a major component of a whole system of taxation of income from capital with taxes effectively levied at different rates across the various industries in the economy.

A third view of the impact of corporation taxation is that the tax is not in fact levied on corporations as such, but on the financial instruments available to companies for financing investment and corporation tax is thus levied on individual claimants on the profits of the company.

When a company is planning an investment project there are a number of ways in which the purchase of capital equipment can be financed. The company can issue shares, it can issue bonds, it can

---

3.19 Harberger's estimates are somewhat sensitive to his particular method of estimation which involves a series of approximation procedures (see J.B. Shoven and J. Whalley 'A general equilibrium calculation of the effects of differential taxation of income from capital in the US', *Journal of Public Economics*, November 1972).

obtain other debt financing, or retain accrued profits over a number of years before the project begins. Dividends on shares will be paid out to shareholders from company profits net of company tax. If, however, debt finance is used as a method of paying back company income to claimants (broadly defined to include bond holders and equity holders), these interest payments are deductible from company profits in determining the corporation tax base.

Of course, a company which was solely interested in minimizing its tax bill would on this reasoning be totally debt financed. In practice, one does not observe this happening for a number of reasons.[20] Companies tend to be acutely tax conscious, but they are also aware that there are major non-tax considerations which enter the debt-equity decision of the company. Increased use of debt financing raises the probability of bankruptcy, which in turn increases the cost of further borrowing should it be required. Merger and takeover threats from other companies tend to become more serious for any company the smaller the equity holding relative to the bond obligations of the company.

Moreover, when the tax treatment within the personal income tax system is taken into account the overall tax position of income as a return to capital becomes even more complicated. A saving in terms of total taxes may be possible for high marginal income tax rate individuals from holding shares in a totally equity financed company (rather than partially equity financed with the individual also holding some bonds issued by the company) which retains corporate profits which, in turn, are paid back[21] to the individual via capital gains. Equity finance with total retention of profits avoids dividend distributions which, in turn, would incur personal income tax liability, a tax liability which cannot be avoided by use of debt finance. It should also be emphasized that with such a strategy non-tax considerations will enter (as with the debt equity decision) through the relative desirability of

---

3.20 It is worth pointing out the relevance here of the extensive economics literature on the so-called Modigliani-Miller theorem. This is a proposition that the value of a firm (the market value of its equity and bond obligations) is independent of the ratio between equity and debt that the firm pursues in its financing policy. It is interesting to note that the original Modigliani-Miller proposition was formalized in a model where corporate taxation was ignored and supposedly substantiated by empirical fact. Given the treatment mentioned of interest payments in the corporation tax system, far from supporting the Modigliani-Miller proposition the data run counter to it as the tax provisions attaching to equity and debt financing should make the value of the firm sensitive to ratio of equity to debt financing. (See M. Miller and F. Modigliani, 'The cost of capital, corporation finance, and the theory of investment' *American Economic Review* 1958 pp. 261-97).
3.21 See footnote 1 page 35, and footnote 2 page 33.

investment projects internal and external to the company, the ease with which income can really be paid back via capital gains, and so on.

These matters are extremely complex and circumstances will vary considerably from firm to firm and it may be a little misplaced for economists to seek to generalize on the position faced by typical firms with typical stockholders. Nevertheless these issues of financial policy are clearly important in an assessment of the impact of corporation tax on the economy.[22] Changes in the financial policies of firms as legal rates of corporation taxation change can substantially alter the effective rates of total taxation on companies and the claimants on the returns to capital.

Thus, those who stress this complex approach would argue that the financial structure of companies will tend to change as corporation tax rates change, and this seriously affects the validity of calculations of the efficiency losses in the economy from the distortionary effects of corporate taxes such as those conducted for the US economy by Harberger and reported as above.

The relevance of tax induced changes in corporate financial policies may be illustrated[23] by an examination of the figures for UK publicly quoted companies for long-term loans as a percentage of shareholders interest via the net worth position of these same companies. Before 1965 in the UK no separate system of corporation tax existed and so there was no double taxation of dividends (once as company profits and once as personal income) as operates with a classical corporation tax system and an income tax system. From 1965 to 1973 a classical corporation tax system prevailed in the UK. Thus taking the pre-1965 regime relative to that post-1965 there is a smaller tax incentive for debt financing. The figures for selected years are; 1961 – 15.1%; 1963 – 15.3%; 1964 – 16.3%; 1965 – 17.4%; 1966 – 20.5%; 1967 – 23.9%; 1968 – 25.9%; 1969 – 26.5% – clearly demonstrating the empirical significance of the financial structure of companies for corporation tax purposes.

3.22 See J. Stiglitz 'Taxation, corporate financial policy, and the cost of capital' *Journal of Public Economics*, February 1973, who uses this approach to suggest that the effects of corporation tax may not be dissimilar to a lump sum tax. This contrasts markedly with the Harberger view discussed earlier.

3.23 The figures given are from 'Company Tax Systems in OECD member countries' OECD, 1973, p. 87. The illustrative nature of the calculations is to be stressed as the figures refer to long-term rather than total debt. Payments of interest on both long and short-term debt on an industrial basis are unfortunately not available in the published social statistics (a situation which hopefully will be remedied). The figures given provide a guide to true movements in debt-equity ratios only in so far as the maturity structure of corporate debt has tended to remain unchanged as tax rates have varied.

Those writers who stress the importance of the financial policy of corporations, when examining the domestic impact of corporation tax arrangements, thus emphasize the complexity of the situation faced by most companies when planning their response to tax changes. That the conclusions of the shifting and general equilibrium approaches can be queried via such analysis would not seem in doubt; what is unfortunately lacking is firm empirical evidence on the strength of these effects.

D Company taxation and risk-bearing

A final view put forward by some economists on the impact of corporation taxation on domestic companies focuses on the impact of corporation taxation on risk taking. This is, in fact, part of a more general issue of the impact on risk taking of all kinds of taxation such as capital gains and personal income taxation. However, it is sometimes suggested in popular debate that taxes on companies represent taxes on the return to risk-taking, and that such taxes might act as a disincentive to companies to take risk and hence be undesirable.

Whether or not this is so is a complex matter depending both on preferences towards risk on the part of both the private and institutional investors in the economy and on the extent of loss-offset provisions in the corporate tax code.[24]

With complete loss-offset[25] in the corporation tax system the government may be thought of as sharing in the risk of any project undertaken in the private sector of the economy provided that companies have profits against which to set losses. The crucial factor is the behaviour of companies to the private (companywide) risk incurred. If private risk[26] (i.e. the dispersion of the net of tax return to any

3.24 See E.D. Domar and R. Musgrave 'Proportional Income Taxation and Risk Bearing' *Quarterly Journal of Economics*, 1944; and J.E. Stiglitz 'Effect of wealth and profits taxation on risk taking' *Quarterly Journal of Economics*, 1969.

3.25 That is losses from one venture can be completely offset against profits of another and unused losses can be carried forward.

3.26 There is a considerable literature on the measurement and quantification of this risk. For purposes of the discussion here, one may think of a company as facing a choice between various ventures each of which has *(ex ante)* a variable outcome. The set of outcomes with the associated probabilities which are attached (either subjectively or objectively) may be represented by a density function of returns. To quantify risk it is convenient to represent such a function

venture) is unchanged when a corporation tax is introduced from the risk incurred with no tax, then social risk-taking (the community's risk on the gross of tax return) will have increased and this may be an inefficient allocation of risk-bearing in the economy with too much risk-taking being undertaken.

Loss-offset provisions in practice tend to be somewhat limited in scope and the analysis of actual corporation tax arrangements on risk-taking is somewhat more complicated than that presented above. This treatment of the impact of corporation tax has not, however, received as much attention as those approaches mentioned earlier and the limited coverage given to this topic here is a reflection of this fact.

It may be remarked in conclusion to this chapter that economists (as on many matters) display a divergence of views on the impact of domestic company taxation arrangements on domestic economic activity. Distinguishing between the competing elements within these views on a solid empirical basis is not yet possible given the limited empirical knowledge available. The approaches outlined in this chapter, however, are of considerable relevance to the more complicated world of multinational (as against domestic) enterprise and will be taken up later on.

---

by an analytic functional form and a two parameter (normal) distribution is often assumed. In such cases risk may be measured by the variance of the standardized normal distribution. Normality as an assumption in such circumstances has been criticized as inappropriate as it attaches finite probabilities to large losses, and some authors have suggested the use of a truncated normal distribution which somewhat complicates the measure of risk.

4. How does international double taxation arise?

This chapter will be devoted to explaining in principle the respects in which international income flows would be subjected to double taxation in the absence of double taxation relief, and outlining the three principal types of relief: by way of exemption, by way of credit and by way of deduction.

A Distinction between economic double taxation and international double taxation

In any discussion of the tax treatment of multinational companies it is important to distinguish two types of double taxation. The term 'economic double taxation' is used to describe the phenomena of an income flow being subjected to more than one charge to tax under the *same* domestic tax system. An example of this is the taxation of distributed company profits under the three principal systems of corporation tax outlined in chapter 2. 'International double taxation' describes the phenomenon of a profit[1] being subjected to more than one charge to tax because that profit would (apart from relieving provisions) be within charge to tax under the system of two or more countries.[2] The ways in which international double taxation is mitigated either by provisions in the tax code of a particular country or by double taxation treaties between states is of crucial importance to multinational enterprises.

4.1 The authors regard the income accruing to a company and the dividend distributed out of that income as being the profit for these purposes.
4.2 i.e. national tax jurisdictions; we are not concerned here with the relations between different tax authorities within national boundaries, such as the relations between the West German länder and federal tax authorities.

B   Principal causes of international double taxation

1   Dual residence

International double taxation[3] can arise where the same taxpayer is resident for tax purposes in two or more countries at the same time. Thus a company resident in two countries both of which levy tax on the basis of residence would be liable to a full charge to corporation tax in each country in the absence of some relief against international double taxation. A company may be resident in two countries at the same time where each country applies the same test for determining residence and applying that test the company is resident in both countries. A company may also have dual residence because the two countries concerned have different tests for determining residence and each country regards the company as resident applying its test.

2   Where the taxable source is situated in one country and the taxpayer is resident in another country

Double taxation also occurs where a taxpayer is resident for tax purposes in one country, while the source of his income is located in another country. In general, systems of taxation levy tax if either the taxpayer or the source of his income is located in the country concerned. The following is a very simple example of this. Company A is resident in state I and carries on a trade in state II through a branch located in state II.[4] Under the tax code of state II, trading profits of branches located in the state are taxed and the state I tax code levies tax on all the profits (both domestic and foreign) of companies resident there. In this case, if there is no double taxation relief, the profits of the trade carried on by the branch located in state II will be subject to full taxation in both states. The possible forms of double tax relief are discussed below.

A more complex case where double taxation arises and which particularly affects multinational enterprises is where a parent company trades abroad through a subsidiary company. Suppose company A is resident in state I and it owns a subsidiary, company B, resident in state

---

4.3 Hereafter the expression 'double taxation' means international double taxation; cases where this is not so will be indicated in the text.
4.4 This example is based on the assumption that state II does not treat a payment by the branch to the company as a dividend. If the tax code of state II deems such payments to be dividends then the same problems would arise as in the case of a parent receiving a dividend from a foreign subsidiary. These are discussed in the following paragraph.

II. Company B carries on a trade in state II and out of its trading profits pays a dividend to company A which in turn pays a dividend to the shareholders in company A, who are resident in state I. Suppose further that the tax codes of both states provide that tax shall be chargeable if either the taxpayer or the source of income is located in that state, and, to keep the example simple, that each state has a classical system of corporation tax. In the absence of relief against double taxation, the following tax charges will arise:

(i) Company B will be liable to corporation tax in state II on its trading profits because both taxpayer and source are located there.

(ii) When company B pays a dividend to company A that dividend will be liable to tax in state II, on the ground that the source, namely the shareholding in company B, is located in state II.

(iii) Company A will be liable to corporation tax in state I on the dividend received from company B because this dividend is part of the income of company A which is a resident of state I.

(iv) The dividend paid by company A out of this income will be subject to state I personal income tax in the hands of the recipient shareholders because they are resident in state I.

Thus in the absence of any double taxation relief, the total burden of tax in this case would be two charges to corporation tax and two charges to tax in respect of dividends. As we saw in chapter 2, in a domestic situation this burden of taxation would not normally arise because of franked investment income or group income provisions. If company A and company B were both resident in the UK, the effect of the UK group income provisions would be that only one amount of corporation tax and only one amount of personal income tax would be exacted from this income flow. This is clearly an argument in favour of having double taxation relief to reduce the burden of taxation which would otherwise be borne by multinational companies. The arguments for and against the various forms of double taxation relief will be examined later. The treatment of international intercorporate dividends will be dealt with more fully in chapter 7.

3 Differences in the computation of profit

Double taxation can arise by reason of countries having different concepts of what constitutes profit for tax purposes or, even though they have the same basic rules for computation of profit, by reason of their interpreting the facts of a given case differently. An example of the latter arises in the case of the powers which the Revenue authorities have in many countries to adjust inter-corporate prices in order to prevent transfer pricing.[5] Two countries may each have a provision in their tax code enabling the Revenue authorities to adjust inter-corporate prices to the market price for the goods or services concerned and to levy tax on the basis that the market price was paid. The Revenue authorities of the two countries may reach different conclusions as to what is the market price for the goods or services concerned and as a result the same profit may be taxed twice.

C   The distinction between bilateral and multilateral tax treaties

A bilateral tax treaty is one made between two countries in order to modify the double taxation which would otherwise arise under their domestic tax provisions. A multilateral tax treaty means one entered into by three or more countries containing common double tax provisions designed to relieve double taxation which would otherwise arise under their respective domestic tax provisions. At present all the double tax treaties are bilateral. It would obviously be impracticable to have a multilateral treaty covering anywhere near all the countries in the world, but it would be possible for the member countries of the EEC in the future to adopt a multilateral tax treaty. The EEC Commission has made a move in this direction in the form of the Draft Directive concerning the harmonization of systems of company taxation and of withholding taxes on dividends.[6]

D   Distinction between bilateral and unilateral relief against double taxation

Bilateral relief is relief granted under arrangements made between two states, normally in the form of a treaty. Each state agrees to grant the reliefs stated in the treaty because the other state will grant reciprocal reliefs. Unilateral relief means relief which one state grants irrespective of whether any reciprocal relief is granted by any other state. Unilateral

---

4.5 That is the name given to the device of selecting artificially high or low prices for goods or services supplied by one company to another company in the same multinational group with the object of causing the profit to arise in one country rather than another.

4.6 This draft directive was transmitted to the Council by the Commission on 1 August 1975. It will be discussed in detail in chapter 13.

reliefs will be contained in the tax code of the state granting the relief. Unilateral relief and bilateral relief can take the form of an exemption, credit or deduction.

E   Exemption, credit and deduction systems of double tax relief

There are three principal methods of relieving double taxation:

1   The exemption system

Under this system the profit is taxed in only one of the states concerned and is exempted from tax in the others. The profit may be exempt from tax in the state of source (exemption on an origin basis) or exempt from tax in the state where the recipient resides (exemption on a destination basis).

Take, for example, the case where a company resident in state I operates abroad through a branch in state II and an exemption system of double taxation is in force between the two states under which trading profits of branches are taxed in the state where the branch is located and are exempt from tax in the other state; i.e. an exemption on a destination basis. The trading profits of the branch would be liable to tax in state II and would be exempt from tax in state I. There is a variant of the exemption system known as 'the system of exemption with progression'.[7] The broad effect of the system of exemption with progression is that although the foreign source income is exempt from taxation in the destination country that foreign source income is aggregated with the taxpayer's other income for the purposes of calculating the progressive rates applicable to his domestic income in the destination country.

2   The credit system

Under this system the tax paid in one state is allowed as a credit against tax liability in the other state. For instance, in the situation postulated above, if states I and II operated a credit system under which tax in the country of source is a credit against tax liability in the country of residence, the branch profits would be liable to tax in state II and that tax would be allowable as a credit against the company's liability to tax in

---

4.7 The system of exemption with progression is considered further in chapter 10.

state I. An obvious feature of a credit system is that the taxpayer ends up paying whichever is the higher of the rates of tax in the states concerned. The credit system has been criticised on these grounds *inter alia*. The UK for instance operates a credit system of double taxation relief in respect of profits of foreign branches and dividend flows from foreign subsidiaries. The view of the UK Revenue is that the object of double taxation relief is to eliminate double taxation and this is achieved if the taxpayer pays no more than the higher of the two rates. Against this it can be objected that the purpose of double taxation relief may not simply be to eliminate double taxation, but also to adopt a system which will promote efficiency and be regarded as fair. These are points which will be discussed in chapters 5 and 6.

3   The deduction system

Under this system the foreign tax is allowed as a deduction from the profit liable to tax in the state concerned. Thus the distinction between this system and the credit system is that under this system the foreign tax is deducted from the tax base, whereas under the credit system the foreign tax is a credit against tax liability. The deduction system will give less relief than the other two systems, but it does at least prevent the total burden of taxes imposed by the states concerned exceeding 100%. Musgrave, for instance, has recently proposed a deduction system for the USA.[8]

4.8 P.B. Musgrave op.cit.

5. An outline of the international taxation of multinational enterprises

In chapter 2 the major features and some details of the methods used to tax domestic companies in various economies have been outlined and in chapter 4 the ways in which international double taxation can arise was discussed. In this chapter a simplified overview of the resulting international tax position of multinational enterprises is presented, and we expand on this in more detail later. The purpose of this chapter is to present an initial summary of the broad features involved so that the following detailed chapters will be placed in their appropriate context.

A Portfolio v. direct foreign investment income and the position of multinational enterprises

A distinction which it is important to clarify is that between portfolio and direct foreign investment income, a distinction which was initially raised in chapter 1. The operations of multinational enterprises result ultimately in across border flows of capital income which in turn yield the parent company direct (as against portfolio) foreign investment income.

Across border flows of investment income in general occur where the claimant (be they a person or a company) who is ultimately entitled to the profits (or losses) of a business venture resides in a country (the destination country) other than the one where the venture is undertaken (the origin country). These activities may be organised in the origin country through a number of possible business forms. For instance, an individual resident in country I may invest in a company operating and incorporated in country II which is undertaking a venture. If any profits accruing to the stockholders in the company in II were to be distributed, the company would have corporation tax liability only in country II. This is the typical situation in the case of portfolio foreign investment income where the dividend paying agent is a company in one country and the dividend receiving agent is an individual resident in another country. This portfolio foreign investment income position may be contrasted with the direct foreign investment income position of a multinational undertaking. Consider the case of an individual resident in country I, who now buys stock in a company also resident and incorporated in country I (instead of II as above). Instead of the individual making an investment in country II via a company in that country, suppose now that it is the company in country I, instead, which makes that investment. This can be done in one of two[1] ways; by establishing a branch in country II which represents the interests of the company in country II, profits being remitted to the company in I through the branch in II; or by establishing a separate company in country II (a subsidiary) owned and controlled by the parent in I, profits being remitted by way of an inter-company dividend.

Whichever of these options is chosen a distinguishing characteristic relative to the case of portfolio foreign investment income is that, assuming these profits are distributed to the parent, the company in I is now effectively liable for corporate taxes in both countries on its branch or subsidiary profits. This is the typical case of direct foreign investment income where the initial receiving agent of investment income flowing across a border is a company rather than a person; the parent company through its ownership of stock in the subsidiary company or control of branch profits effectively incurs corporate tax liability in both countries I and II (either on the branch profits, or the subsidiary profits).[2]

The double taxation issue which arises with multinational enterprises is thus a matter of double corporate tax liability and the multinational enterprise taxation problem involves, in its simplest form, the total taxation of a parent company in one country and a branch or subsidiary company in another country.

5.1 Here we make the simplifying assumption that no tax or other inducements cause the operation to be conducted through a third or even fourth country. It is apparent that these matters can very quickly become overly complicated, and so lesser degree complications of this form will only be brought into the discussion where they are relevant.

5.2 It is, however, worth making the point that in the UK (as in the USA) branch profits are taxed as they accrue, whereas subsidiary profits are (typically) only taxed as they are distributed.

B Origin country taxes – corporate taxes and dividend witholding taxes

As stated in chapter 2 most market economies have domestic corporation tax systems. Typically, origin country operations of multinational enterprises (whether through subsidiaries or branches) will therefore come under charge to the origin country corporation tax. There are, of course, important differences in the structure of the tax from country to country (the classical, two-rate and imputation systems being the most common), and where similar taxation structures prevail there are differences in tax rates and in the details of the determination of the tax base (capital allowances in particular differ).[3]

A further feature of the origin country tax position of multinational enterprises is that a number of countries have witholding of personal income taxes on dividends at source administered directly by companies and also withholding taxes on interest and royalties.[4] To complicate matters further some of these taxes are not called witholding taxes as such within the context of the income tax system, but it is important to point out that they effectively[5] operate as such. This point of what is legally and what is in effect (if not legally) a dividend withholding tax is important when we come to consider the effects of

---

5.3 In addition, they are typically (and importantly) only granted on an origin basis. If a UK company's branch invests in plant abroad the 100% first year depreciation in the UK is not granted.

5.4 For instance, in West Germany the rate at present is 25%.

5.5 A prime example of this last point is the UK, where before 1973 withholding at source by companies of personal income tax at the basic rate of income tax on dividends operated; taxes withheld by a company making a distribution which were then paid directly to the tax authorities. Under the new UK imputation corporation tax system, withholding taxes of this form no longer operate but a company making a dividend distribution in the UK is required to make a payment of Advanced Corporation Tax (ACT). At the same time a tax credit is given to the recipient shareholder with the credit acting as an advance payment of personal income tax, such that a basic rate taxpayer is liable for no further income tax on the dividend received. Although not directly labelled as such, to the extent that ACT paid by a company provides a credit against personal income tax for recipient shareholders it may be regarded as having the same effect as a dividend withholding tax. It is, however, important to emphasize that ACT is not in law a dividend withholding tax. This is most important for consideration of the role of double taxation treaties in cases involving the UK as origin country as is stressed below in the text. The situation in the UK was made even more complicated with an increase (by 50%) in ACT with no increase in the credit to recipient shareholders so that not all of ACT was to be regarded as a dividend withholding tax.

double taxation treaties which attempt mutually to reduce dividend withholding taxes. Double taxation treaties focus rather narrowly on legally defined dividend withholding taxes so that, for instance, the situation at present in the UK is disadvantageous to foreign subsidiaries operating in the UK relative to the pre–1973 position when dividend withholding taxes were differently treated.

Thus, if we consider activity undertaken abroad by a subsidiary company of a multinational enterprise with the parent company in a destination country, the tax treatment in the origin country of the income accruing to the subsidiary company typically will be along the following lines. If the operation abroad is organised through a foreign subsidiary company as we suppose here, that subsidiary company will typically pay origin country corporate taxes on profits, and then also pay withholding taxes on dividends remitted to the parent company. In addition, there may also be withholding taxes on payments of interest from the subsidiary company to the parent company; and in some countries withholding taxes on royalties. As a reasonably accurate simplification of this overall position then, we may think of a combined origin country tax on the whole of a multinational operation organised through a subsidiary as consisting of two parts corporate taxes on profits of the subsidiary and a range of withholding taxes (on dividends, interest and royalties) on sums remitted back to the parent company.

Where an operation abroad is organized through a branch[6] rather than through a subsidiary company no intercompany dividend will be involved in any remittance and depending on the countries involved withholding taxes on dividends may not be levied. Some countries treat payments from branches to parents as dividends for the purposes of determining withholding tax liability and a multinational enterprise may suffer a withholding tax on branch profits in the origin country, but this treatment would seem to be the exception rather than the rule. In the UK, payments made from branches to parent companies abroad are not treated as dividends, in fact, in Western Europe in only one country are branch profits remitted to a foreign parent company treated as dividends.

There are additional differences in tax treatment between branches and subsidiary companies and it is usually suggested that the balance of taxation advantage is such that most multinational activity is conducted

---

5.6 For an excellent discussion on the concept and operation of branches (permanent establishments) see M.B. Ludwig *General Report* (on permanent establishments) given to the 27th Conference of the International Fiscal Association, Lausanne, 1973.

abroad through subsidiary companies.[7] Belgium, for instance, has higher corporate tax rates on branch profits accruing to a foreign parent company than on profits of domestic or subsidiary companies. Branch operation may also render both the parent and the branch liable to tax in each country on the world-wide profits of the entire company. This is, however, an extremely rare situation, particularly in those cases where double taxation treaties exist between countries.

As a general picture of the tax situation of multinational enterprises in origin countries, one can think of the major portion of multinational activity as being organized through subsidiary companies. The subsidiary companies are liable to corporation tax on profits of the subsidiary company under the origin country's corporate tax system and also dividend (and interest and royalty) withholding taxes on dividends (interest and royalties) remitted to the parent company. This distinction between the two components of origin country taxes is important in considering reliefs given to reduce the overall tax burden on multinational enterprise.

5.7 This is a commonly expressed view that has passed into conventional wisdom but the UK statistics seem to be somewhat contradictory. Two sources of statistics are now available in the UK: a survey of 1,000 companies with 'significant overseas investments' carried out each year by the Department of Industry and reported in their Business Monitor series (see M4, *Overseas Transactions*, April 1973), and an analysis of company tax returns published by the Inland Revenue (see Table 36, 'Income from Abroad', *Inland Revenue Statistics* 1974). The Department of Industry report world-wide net profits of branches of UK companies in 1971 as £110.6 million and world-wide net profits of subsidiaries (and associates) of UK parent companies in 1971 as £563.7 million. The Inland Revenue report for financial year 1971–2 the case IV and case V income (primarily subsidiary dividends and interest payments) from abroad as assessed to companies as £415.0 million and a case I schedule D figure (particular kinds of branch operations) on net trading profits from abroad as £1,017.2 million. The discrepancy on the subsidiary figures is partially accounted for by remittances in the Inland Revenue figures versus world-wide profits in the Department of Industry figures, although the Department of Industry report a figure for 1971 that only 44% of subsidiary profits are remitted so that one might have expected if anything a larger discrepancy. The discrepancy between the branch figures causes more problems and cannot be accounted for by the remittance versus world-wide basis. It would seem that operations of certain companies on a world-wide basis are organized from the UK without being linked to a definable UK parent company which has other trading activities in the UK. These would appear to be excluded from the Department of Industry figures but enter into the Inland Revenue figures (although a considerable portion of branch activity linked to UK trading concerns does not enter). The Inland Revenue figures, do, however, suggest that the conventional view (at least for UK based concerns) of activity abroad being conducted primarily through subsidiary activity may merit some re-examination.

C   Destination country taxes – the role of credits, exemptions and double taxation treaties

A typical multinational operation will thus involve the generation of profit in an origin country which we will assume is (ultimately) paid to the parent through an origin country subsidiary company. The subsidiary company will have paid origin country corporation tax and (when repatriated via dividends) dividend withholding taxes on the profits which it makes. This net of origin country tax profit remitted by the subsidiary company then comes under the tax system of the destination country in the hands of the parent company.

The destination country will typically have a corporation tax to which the profit received by the parent company will be liable. Furthermore, if a dividend distribution is then made to stockholders in the parent company out of this profit received from abroad, liability to personal income tax on the part of stockholders may also arise. This personal income tax may be collected in whole or in part by a withholding tax at source on dividend distributions.

As we have already stated most developed countries have some system of reliefs in these situations to avoid or at least reduce what would otherwise be a double tax liability on the profit flow, i.e. one payment to each country's tax authority.[8] The justification for these reliefs will be discussed in the next chapter, but the broad principle may be compared to that embodied in some domestic corporate tax systems that those dividends which represent flows of funds between companies (i.e. flows internal to the corporate sector) should not be further taxed under the corporation tax. In the UK, for instance, there are the franked investment income provisions under which a dividend received by a holding company from a subsidiary company bears no further corporation taxes. A multinational operation is viewed in some countries[9] in a similar light to a purely domestic corporate transaction and the corporate sector is thus treated from the point of view of the destination country's tax authorities as extending into foreign lands. Even though the dividend flow occurs across a national border the principle of not further taxing flows internal to the corporate sector is still taken to apply. As with all systems of reliefs, the actual arrangements which operate in destination countries are complicated.

5.8 As natural as this may seem, Sweden, for instance, did not introduce such a system on a universal basis until 1967 (see M. Norr, C. Sandels and N. Hornhammer: *The Tax System in Sweden*, p. 60).
5.9 Most notably in Holland.

Reliefs can be bilateral (i.e. restricted to flows between pairs of countries) or unilateral (i.e. given by one country independently of the other country involved) given on a credit or on an exemption basis, and (at least in theory) administered on a destination country or origin country basis. We have attempted to provide some summary information on the position in individual countries in an appendix to this chapter.

There are two major choices that one can identify as having to be faced by most countries in deciding between the groups of principles under which unilateral reliefs may be administered. The first is the choice between the credit and the exemption principle of administering unilateral relief (a relief, in practice, given in all major countries).[10] The credit principle gives relief from tax liability in the destination country for taxes actually paid in the origin country; a direct crediting of taxes paid in one locality against taxes to be paid elsewhere is thus involved. The exemption system exempts income which has already been taxed in an origin country from further tax in the destination country. A feature which could further complicate this position is that unilateral reliefs could be administered (although, in practice this does not happen)[11] on an origin country basis instead of a destination country basis. In this case, an origin country would give relief from double taxation based on taxes which are due to be paid by multinational enterprises in the destination country. A destination country relief (the usual practice) gives relief based on taxes which have been paid in the origin country.

To illustrate the broad features of this structure further we may take a simple example of a company operating in two countries I and II with total domestic tax rates on corporate income in each country of t_I and t_{II}. To keep this illustration of the principles clear the complications of separate components of company taxes and also dividend withholding taxes are avoided. Table 1 then lists the tax liabilities in each country under each of the alternative systems that might be operated. In addition to a system of unilateral reliefs from double taxation (which in practice, each major country operates), systems of bilateral tax treaties also exist between many pairs of nations. Typically, double

5.10 It has been suggested by Musgrave (P.B. Musgrave op. cit.) that to counteract advantages which US parent companies obtain elsewhere in the tax system (which will be discussed later) that no double tax relief at all should be granted to US based multinational companies, but instead foreign taxes should just be deductible from profits in determining tax liability in the US. This point is taken up more fully in the next chapter.
5.11 At one time a system along these lines was in operation in Italy; we are grateful to Professor J. van Hoorn for this point.

taxation treaties are negotiated on a bilateral basis[12] (involving two countries only). The simple example above involves only two countries and bilateral and multilateral arrangements in this particular case will coincide. These treaties often state that country I agrees to treat differently dividends flowing abroad to country II from those distributed domestically or to other countries (taxing at a lower rate $\bar{t} <$ t_I) if, in return, country II also agrees to give similar treatment to dividends flowing to I (typically taxing them at the same rate $\bar{t} < t_{II}$). With a few exceptions bilateral treaties are of this reciprocal form (similarity in provisions independent of the direction of profit flow). Bilateral double taxation treaties typically exist in addition to unilateral reliefs, and, in practice, grant bilateral reductions in withholding tax rates on interest and dividends, tax rates on royalties, as well as providing definitions of terms and provisions to exchange information between tax authorities. No double taxation treaty exists, to our

Table 1

Credit and exemption relief on dividend flows between subsidiary and parent companies—no tax treaties

	Country I Tax rate t_I	Country II Tax rate t_{II}
Total tax rate on profits arising if there is:	*Dividend flow from I to II*	*Dividend flow from II to I*
1. Exemption on origin basis	t_{II}	t_I
2. Exemption on destination basis	t_I	t_{II}
3. Credit relief on source basis	$\max(t_I, t_{II})$	$\max(t_I, t_{II})$
4. Credit relief on destination basis	$\max(t_I, t_{II})$	$\max(t_I, t_{II})$

5.12 The 1963 OECD model treaty which forms the basis for many of the double taxation treaties which exist, if adopted by every pair of countries on the same basis would effectively provide a multilateral system of treaties. It is, of course, most unlikely that such treaties would be adopted between developed and developing countries (almost totally origin countries in all transactions in which they are involved). This is borne out in practice.

knowledge, which bilaterally reduces the rate of corporation tax (rather than withholding taxes) applied to branch profits or profits of subsidiary companies of foreign parent companies.

The typical multinational enterprise thus encounters liability to corporation tax in destination countries in addition to tax liability encountered in origin countries. Unilateral relief from double taxation for multinational companies is given for corporate and other underlying taxes in all countries almost solely on a destination basis. This relief may be administered on an exemption or credit basis. In addition bilateral relief through double taxation treaties for dividend and interest withholding taxes is given in a large number of cases involving particular pairs of countries. Treaty reliefs unlike unilateral reliefs are usually administered on an origin country basis. By way of illustration of these reliefs the UK and the US give unilateral relief for corporate and other underlying taxes on a credit basis;[13] while Holland, France and Brazil give relief on an exemption basis.[14] Double taxation treaties exist between most pairs of industrialized countries,[15] with treaty agreed withholding tax rates of between 5% and 15%, administered on an origin basis. Most of the taxes described earlier as dividend withholding taxes are thus regarded for the purpose of these double taxation agreements. Further information on these arrangements is provided in an appendix to this chapter.

D   Destination and origin country taxes – complications with systems of corporation tax

The discussion in the previous sections of this chapter has been concerned with situations where single rate corporation taxes exist in

---

5.13 The US allows as an alternative aggregation of all tax payments on all foreign income before the credit is taken whereas the UK treats each case separately on a country by country basis. For a company receiving dividends from both high and low tax areas the US averaging provisions can represent a considerable benefit.

5.14 More detail on the overall position in a number of countries is provided in an appendix to this chapter. For certain countries different types of transactions are treated in different ways and the adoption of a single label credit or exemption for these countries may be less informative even though such labels are used in table 1.

5.15 In the enlarged nine country European Community there are seventy-two pairs of countries and only in four cases do double tax treaties at present not exist: Ireland and Italy, Ireland and Luxembourg, Denmark and Luxembourg and Italy and Luxembourg.

each of the destination and origin countries. From chapter 2 this will be recognised as a case where a classical single rate system of corporation tax operates in each country. In practice, some countries operate imputation or two-rate systems[16] of corporation tax and an important difference between these two forms of corporate taxation is in the tax treatment of dividends paid abroad.

In the case of two-rate systems of corporation tax a lower tax rate is charged on distributions than on retentions and where payment of a dividend is made by a subsidiary company to a parent company in a destination country with a classical system of corporation tax and a credit double taxation relief system, a considerable amount of further tax will usually be paid.[17] If however, an exemption system of double taxation relief exists in the destination country, the multinational parent will in all likelihood be taxed on a more favourable basis than a domestic company in the destination country if the saving in corporation tax through the two-rate system abroad more than compensates for the dividend withholding tax liability. On these grounds one might think that two-rate corporate tax systems such as in West Germany would tend to be accompanied by a series of double taxation treaties allowing that country higher dividend withholding tax rates than average. In practice (i.e. in the German case) this does not seem to be so; dividend withholding tax rates of 15% are typical in West German double taxation treaties as against a norm in the range of 5%–15% for other countries in their double taxation agreements.

In the case of a country with an imputation corporation tax system a single tax rate is effectively charged on all corporate profits whether distributed or not, as under a classical system corporation tax. The tax on distributed corporate profits, however, is typically composed of two components. One is a payment for which credit is given to stockholders for personal income tax liability incurred on dividends received. The other is a component bringing the total tax liability up to that rate which is charged on retained profits.

5.16 At present the German system is two-rate with a 51% rate on retained profits and 15% on distributed profits. A commitment has been made by the government to move to a split-rate imputation system with rates of 56% on retentions and 36% on distributions, part of the tax on distributions being imputable against personal income tax liability. This new system is supposedly to be introduced in January 1977, although the current indications would seem to be that this is unlikely.

5.17 This argument is based on the fact that destination country tax rate is commonly higher than the country distribution tax rate plus the extra withholding tax (if any).

This system also raises difficulties in connection with the tax treatment of multinational enterprises as the UK case illustrates. Double tax relief for taxes paid on dividends received from subsidiary companies operating abroad with a domestic parent in the UK, even in the event of total distribution to resident shareholders by the parent company, is effectively only usable against the reduced rate (in the UK called mainstream) corporation tax liability of the parent company in the UK. If corporate tax rates abroad (perhaps in a classical system country) are higher than this reduced rate (as is typically true) then domestic companies can be considered to be treated far more lightly than domestic based multinational companies. In the context of the UK system this is part of a range of issues sometimes referred to as the overspill problem; the accumulation of large amounts of credits for foreign taxes paid which more than meet domestic corporate tax liability.[18]

A second set of problems faced by multinational operations arising from the operation of the imputation system of corporation tax, is whether the credit given is refundable across the countries when the credit is received by a parent company abroad rather than a resident domestic shareholder. Related to this is the treatment of the tax credit from the point of view of double taxation treaties. This is a problem which at the present time is of particular importance for the situation in the UK and France, being the two major EEC countries operating imputation systems. Replacement of a classical system by an imputation system typically involves a higher tax rate on retentions to preserve the yield from the tax. If the imputation tax credit is not given under double taxation treaties to foreign parent companies, then the subsidiary of a foreign parent will in effect finish up paying the tax rate charged on retained profits plus the withholding tax rate on dividends even though a dividend distribution will have been made. The recent move from a classical system to an imputation system in the UK having been accompanied by an increase in the corporation tax rate from 40% to 52%, foreign subsidiary companies operating in the UK can justifiably

---

5.18 The importance of this problem depends on the magnitude of the tax rates involved. In the case of the UK it has been claimed by some of the companies affected that they pay tax abroad at a rate on average of 45–50% and so a move in the UK to an imputation system with a mainstream rate of 19% on distributions and ACT of 33% (1974 tax rates) puts them at quite a severe disadvantage relative to domestic companies. Figures recently published by the Inland Revenue (see *Inland Revenue Statistics 1974*, table 29) indicate that this figure of an average tax rate of 45–50% may not be too far off the mark.

claim to have been placed at a relative disadvantage[19] compared to the earlier position.

In these circumstances a multinational parent company will have substantial credits for personal income tax liability in the country where the subsidiary company operates; but because the subsidiary company will typically be largely or wholly owned by the parent company few or none of its shareholders will have any such personal income tax liability in the origin country against which to use the credits. These credits will be effectively useless to the subsidiary company. The UK, furthermore, does not regard a payment of ACT as a dividend withholding tax for the purpose of double taxation agreements which has led to considerable dissatisfaction among foreign subsidiaries operating in the UK.

Thus the systems of corporation tax adopted by various countries along with the interpretations placed on various components of the tax arrangements involved can further complicate the broad picture of the tax treatment of multinational enterprises outlined in earlier sections.

This chapter has sought to provide an overview of the international tax position of multinational enterprises. It should be clear that it is difficult (and sometimes dangerous) to generalise in these matters and this overview has been provided in full knowledge that much elaboration on this will be necessary. This we attempt in following chapters by providing more detail on individual components of this overall set of arrangements.

Appendix to chapter 5

Summary of the taxation treatment of inter-company transactions in particular developed countries

In the preceding chapter the taxation position of multinational enterprises has been outlined in schematic terms, often without reference to the actual position in individual countries. This appendix

---

5.19 In the event of dividends being paid to resident shareholders outside the UK in countries with which the UK has double taxation treaties, mutually eliminating income tax on non-residents from each of the other countries' income tax systems a refund of the payment of ACT should be possible. A similar arrangement operates with the French *avoir fiscal* for certain pairs of countries (such as France and the UK). Both the French and the British are quite liberal in their interpretation of an individual by including companies abroad receiving a dividend from a domestic company but which do not have more than a 10% interest in that operation.

Table 2[1]
Systems of tax treatment for multinational enterprises in
the absence of treaty

Country	System[2] of unilateral relief applied to dividend income received by parent company from foreign subsidiary	Rates of withholding tax on dividends, interest and royalties paid by subsidiary company[3] to foreign parent company		
Australia	Credit	30	10	10[5]
Belgium	Credit	20	20	20
Brazil	Exemption	25[4]	25[4]	25
Canada	Credit	25	25	25
France	Exemption	25	25	19.2
Holland	Exemption	25	25	25
Italy	Credit	30	30	14
Japan	Credit	20[6]	20[6]	20[6]
UK	Credit	0[7]	35	35
USA	Credit	30	30	30
West Germany	Credit	25	25	25

1 The documents used include *Taxation of Patent Royalties,
  Dividends, and Interest in Europe* and *Corporate Taxation
  in Latin America* published by the International Bureau for
  Fiscal Documentation, Amsterdam; other information was
  provided by embassies or obtained from recent government documents of the country concerned.
2 The arrangements in each country which are classified by
  such a heading are complex and the labels are chosen even
  though in certain cases different transactions are treated
  in different ways.
3 The rates quoted apply to transactions between a parent
  company and a 100% owned subsidiary.
4 Plus a supplementary tax on 'excess' remittances; see
  source documents for more detail.
5 The tax rate is 42.5% of net income paid with an upper
  limit of 10% of gross income.
6 In 1976 and after a rate of 12% will apply.
7 Advanced corporation tax is not treated here as a withholding tax.

attempts to provide an indication of the position in a number of countries so as to give the reader a broad picture of similarities and differences in arrangements and tax rates. A broad outline cannot cover the particular circumstances of more complicated individual cases and the tables which follow are not intended to serve as up to date guides for practitioners who would be well advised to consult more complete documentary sources. All the information used in the compilation of these tables is from secondary rather than original source material and the dates at which various arrangements reported were in operation differ to some extent.

Table 3[1]

Summary of tax treaties between developed countries as they affect multinational enterprises withholding tax rates on dividends,[2] interest, and royalties

Country of location of subsidiary[3] company	Australia			Belgium			Brazil			Canada			Country of location France		
	D	I	R	D	I	R	D	I	R	D	I	R	D	I	R
Australia	—	—	—	No treaty[4]			No treaty			15	no provision	0	15	10	10
Belgium	No treaty			—	—	—	15	15	10	15	15	10	10	15	0
Brazil[5]	No treaty			15	15	10	—	—	—	No treaty			15	15	15
Canada	15	no provision	0	15	15	10	No treaty			—	—	—	15	15	10
France	15	10	10	10	15	0	15	15	15	15	15	10	—	—	—
Holland	15	10	10	5	10	0	No treaty			0	0	0	5	0	0
Italy	No treaty			15	15	0	No treaty			No treaty			15	15	0
Japan	15	10	10	15	15	10	10	10	10	15	15	15	15	15	10
UK	15	10	10	15	15	0	No treaty			15	15	10	5	10	0
USA	15	no provision	no provision	15	15	0	No treaty			15	15	15	5	10	5
West Germany	15	10	10	15	15	0	15	15	15	15	15	15	25	0	0

1 See note 1 to table 2. An additional source used for this table was *Tax Conventions of Japan* (The Tax Bureau, Ministry of Finance, Japan).
2 Again a 100% holding in any subsidiary company is assumed. For dividend withholding tax rates, and to a lesser extent for interest withholding tax rates, it is not uncommon for a different rate of tax to apply if the equity interest of the parent company is below a certain figure (usually 25%, sometimes 10%, and in the case of the Canadian/Holland treaty 95%). The rates applying where the equity interest is above the qualifying figure are usually lower, treaties involving West Germany being the notable exceptions.

The situation is summarised in two tables. The first reports the system of unilateral relief for income received by parent companies from abroad, and the rates of withholding tax on dividends, interest, and royalties paid abroad to subsidiaries in the absence of any treaty. The second table reports the rates of withholding tax on dividends, interest, and royalties as agreed by treaty between pairs of countries. As different rates can apply to these transactions as circumstances differ, we have concentrated on dividend payments where the parent company has a 100% interest in the subsidiary company, and on interest payments on intercompany loans. Equally, industrial rather than

| parent[3] company | | | | | | | | | | | | | | | | |
| Holland | | | Italy | | | Japan | | | UK | | | USA | | | West Germany | | |
(D)	I	R	D	I	R	D	I	R	D	I	R	D	I	R	D	I	R
5	10	10	No treaty			15	10	10	15	10	10	15	no provision	No provision	15	10	10
5	10	0	15	15	0	15	15	0	15	15	0	15	15		15	15	0
No treaty			No treaty			10	10	10	No treaty			No treaty		0	15	15	15
0	0	0	No treaty			15	15	15	15	15	10	15	15	15	15	15	15
5	10	0	15	15	0	15	15	10	5	10	0	5	10	5	25	0	0
—	—		0	0	10	10	5	10	5	0	0	5	0	0	10	0	0
0	0		—	—	—	10	10	10	5	15	0	5	no provision	0	no provision	0	0
5	10		10	10	10	—	—	—	10	10	10	10	10	10	25	10	10
0	0		5	15	0	10	10	10	—	—	—	15	0	0	15	0	0
0	0		5	no provision	0	10	10	10	15	0	0	—	—		15	0	0
0	0		no provision	0	0	10	10	10	15	0	0	15	0		—	—	—

Generally speaking, treaties are reciprocal in the sense of a similar treatment applying to transactions independent of the direction involved. The Japan/Holland and Japan/West Germany treaties are notable as asymmetric arrangements.

The absence of a treaty does not preclude current negotiations (such as between Belgium and Australia) or a negotiated treaty which remains unratified (such as between the US and Brazil).

Treaties between developed and less developed countries are rare. For instance, countries such as Peru and Argentina each only have one treaty (both with Sweden).

copyright royalties are considered for withholding tax rates on royalties.

The broad picture which emerges from table 1 is of a mixture of exemption and imputation systems with withholding tax rates in the region of 25–30% as common in the absence of treaty. Table 2 presents a more confused picture. In the presence of treaties withholding tax rates typically drop into the range 10–15%. Some countries (e.g. Holland) tend to have lower rates of tax and others tend to have higher rates (such as West Germany on dividends). The relative absence of tax treaties between developed and developing or less developed countries (as emphasized in note 5 to table 2) is a point of some importance.

6. Should there be relief for multinational enterprises from double taxation?

Chapters 4 and 5 have explained how multinational business activity gives rise to a form of double taxation. The nature of this double taxation stems from multinational operations in which intermediaries generate income (profit) through trading in one country for payment to some ultimate dividend recipient in another (eventual) country. The double taxation arises as the origin country first taxes the profit in the hands of the branch or subsidiary company, and the destination country subsequently taxes the remaining profits in the hands of the parent company. In this chapter we examine the justifications which can and have been put forward for operating systems of relief from this double taxation.

By way of qualification of a number of points which will be made in this chapter, the following remarks are offered: Firstly, all major industrialised countries (and to a limited extent some less developed countries) operate systems of relief of one kind or another from this double taxation. In practice, these have evolved in *ad hoc* fashion, and we shall consider the operation of these arrangements more fully later. As these reliefs are a key issue in the whole question of the international taxation of multinational enterprise, we work at this stage in terms of hypothetical (and in some ways unrealistic) situations which do not necessarily refer to any individual country's system. It may also seem to the reader a little pedantic to be preoccupied with justifications for systems which are already in operation. These systems are, however, currently being brought into question (importantly in the USA) and a discussion of the basic rationale for such systems helps put the issues involved in perspective. Secondly, as with most matters that economists consider, things in practice are a good deal more complicated than the sometimes simple abstractions with which they work. In this chapter we consider only simplified cases where profits arise in origin countries, are taxed there, and then repatriated to a destination country where they are further taxed in the hands of a parent company. We also briefly consider some of the complications which arise through deferred repatriation of profits. We ignore for the moment flows of profits from subsidiary companies (or branches) to parent companies which travel via third and even fourth countries. Thirdly, the so-called double taxation of foreign source income (and in particular business income) is by no means the only instance of double taxation that one can identify. Income taxation has been criticized by some economists because of a double taxation of savings; savings being made out of net of tax income with further tax being applied to the income return to invested savings.[1] Classical corporation taxation systems have been criticized as a double taxation of dividends; dividends being paid out of net of corporation tax profits and attracting personal income tax in the hands of dividend recipients. Thus the problem of double taxation is one that is not exclusive to the tax treatment of multinational enterprises.

A   Multinational enterprises and domestic corporation tax systems

In order to consider the justification (or lack of it) for double taxation relief being given to multinational enterprise, it is necessary first to examine the objectives of domestic corporation taxation systems as they relate to transactions between corporations. It was remarked earlier that in broad terms corporation taxes may be seen as a response to a deficiency in the redistributive power of personal income taxes, namely that profits accruing to stockholders in a company are taxed under the personal income tax code on distribution to the shareholder rather than on accrual.

As mentioned earlier, such an argument can only strictly be used to justify an undistributed profits tax rather than a corporation tax; and furthermore it is far from obvious that a sensible response to such a deficiency is to introduce a new tax rather than change the personal income tax system along the lines earlier referred to. Be that as it may, this justification of corporation tax is important for our discussion here in that it draws a sharp dividing line between the personal and corporate

---

6.1 These are the grounds which have been used to support a change from income taxation to an expenditure tax. (See N. Kaldor *An Expenditure Tax*, Allen and Unwin, 1955).

sectors while drawing no such line between companies within the corporate sector.

Thus, it can be stated that the intention of corporation income tax systems is to tax profits originating in the corporate sector of the economy irrespective of the number of companies between which that profit flows in the year. This taxation is in addition to the personal income taxes borne by stockholders on dividend distributions which may be made. From the point of view of multinational enterprises the important part in all of this in terms of their claim to double taxation relief is 'irrespective of the number of companies between which that profit flows'.

We have already seen that most countries have domestic corporation tax systems which either exempt or lightly tax profit flows between domestic companies. In the UK a system of franked investment income and group income relief operates which exempts from further corporate tax profits received by one company net of corporate tax from another domestic company. In the USA 85% of such net of corporate tax profits are exempted in the hands of a receiving company; in Belgium the figure is either 90% or 95% depending upon circumstances; in the Netherlands there is total exemption if the receiving company has a 5% or greater share in the paying company, and so on. All these intercorporate dividend provisions typically apply only to domestic companies[2] and where these arrangements do apply only to domestic companies, then some corresponding provision for multinational companies may be called for.

Thus the issues involved in the tax treatment of multinational enterprises may be thought of as follows: are multinational subsidiary and parent companies to be thought of as companies which are the same as any other domestic companies in the relevant countries; and, if so, are reliefs which keep the taxation borne by profits originating and remaining within the domestic economy to once a year to be granted to profit flows of an international character? The obvious difference from the domestic situation is that although for economic purposes a multinational enterprise may be thought of as a single undertaking, its operations straddle tax regimes and so for tax purposes it has to be disentangled into a number of constituent parts. Which tax authority can claim jurisdiction over which part of the whole operation, even if a partition can be agreed; and how different tax rates charged by different

---

6.2 In the UK these provisions are only applicable to receipts from other domestic companies. In the Netherlands they are extended to receipts from all companies which is the effective way the Dutch exemption system of double tax relief on overseas earnings of companies operates.

tax authorities are to be reconciled, lie at the heart of what is a complex set of issues.

B   Efficiency in resource use

One of the key elements in discussing the justification of the tax treatment of multinational enterprises in terms of tax reliefs is the concept of economic efficiency. Efficiency in the use of resources is one of the basic concepts in economic theory, an efficient allocation being defined as an allocation of resources such that it is not possible to rearrange the use being made of resources to increase one output in an economy without, in turn, reducing any other. This is a requirement that at the margin all resources be equally productive in all alternative uses. As we shall see relief from double taxation for multinational enterprises may be justified on an efficiency argument in terms of the world-wide allocation of resources, but this may (and typically will) conflict with national interest.[3]

Economic efficiency as it relates to the use of capital resources requires that capital receive the same rate of return (i.e. the marginal productivity of capital be equalised) in all possible domestic uses. In a competitive environment within a domestic economy, factors of production will tend to receive their marginal products in all possible uses.

When the problem of the taxation of multinational companies is examined from an efficiency point of view, a tax situation can be described as causing an inefficient allocation of world-wide resources if taxation systems when taken in combination give a differential total tax treatment to capital income depending upon whether or not it flows abroad or whether or not it has been received from abroad. Efficiency of resource use on a world-wide basis requires the same tax treatment (in total) of all capital income in all countries. This would achieve a result of all capital income bearing, in effect, the same tax rate independently of where it is employed or the ultimate recipient resides. If in any country taxes on income from abroad are higher than on income generated domestically, then from a world-wide efficiency viewpoint too little income will flow abroad. The capital funds flowing abroad will earn a higher rate of return gross of tax than the funds employed domestically and world production could be increased by allowing such a capital flow to take place.

6.3 This conflict is taken up in a more formal setting in chapter 12.

While the notion of an efficient use of resources on a world-wide basis has a straightforward conclusion for the tax treatment of multinational enterprises, the prescription is more complex if the maximum national return obtainable from a single country's resources is considered instead. Any domestic tax authority can alter the rate of tax on income flowing abroad, allowing the tax authority to act in the national interest in a way comparable to a monopoly purchaser of foreign capital.

The taxation of multinational enterprise also involves more than one tax authority. Even assuming each tax authority designs its own tax structure so as to pursue an efficient allocation of world resources, the division of the total tax revenue collected between the countries involved is also a matter of critical importance to each country. Suppose country I is the country in which a multinational parent with a subsidiary company in country II operates. Suppose further that countries I and II charge the same rates of corporate tax. By giving a credit in I (the destination country) for taxes paid in II (the origin country), country I may move the overall position closer towards an efficient allocation of resources from a world-wide point of view since the net of tax rate of return of capital in I will be equalized between domestic and foreign uses. Country I, however, receives none of the tax revenue paid in country II and may be able to improve the income return to the whole country (i.e. including tax revenue) by raising its tax on income received from II so that in total such income bears more tax than income earned domestically in I. Such a situation would represent an inefficient allocation of resources from a world-wide stance, but I will have improved its share of the world product. It is this incentive for individual country tax authorities to pursue their own national interest that results in the situation that there are distinct domestic tax treatments for foreign source income each of which may be appropriate from a national viewpoint. As the national interest will take a different form as circumstances differ from country to country, a diversity of tax regimes will develop.

This complication of national versus world-wide interest is such that when asking the question is double taxation relief for multinational enterprise justified, one must ask from whose viewpoint. In terms of maximising total world product (quite apart, that is, from its distribution) relief is by and large fully justified in all cases. This view is sharply qualified when national advantage is taken into account, and in fact the appropriate degree of double tax relief one country should give is not well defined in isolation from the tax rates levied in other countries. This interdependence of decisions between nations is a theme to which we return later. It is also worth pointing out that most developed countries are both recipients and exporters of capital income, and although the issue of double taxation relief is in these cases substantially influenced by the net exporter/recipient position, the reciprocity of the income flows introduces an element of incentive to reach bilateral rather than multilateral agreements. The position is somewhat changed where flows are unidirectional (as between developing and developed nations) and in practice these situations are characterized by an almost total absence of treaty agreements.

C Equity and stabilisation arguments

Two further sets of issues of relevance to the discussion of double taxation relief for multinational enterprises are equity and stabilisation arguments. Equity issues in public finance are concerned with notions of equal treatment. A distinction is normally drawn between horizontal and vertical equity, horizontal equity referring to equal treatment of 'equals' and vertical equity to 'fair' treatment between various groups of 'equals'. Application of these principles to the tax treatment of multinational enterprises is complicated by the definitional problems of 'equality' in such a context. If horizontal equity is interpreted as implying equal treatment between companies whether domestic or multinational then a problem arises as to where the multinational enterprise is thought of as being situated for the equity discussion.[4] It would seem, however, that an absence of double taxation reliefs in this regard can only be justified if no equity comparison at all is made between multinational enterprises and domestic companies, which, of course, may well be appropriate. If, however, one advocates equal treatment of income accruing to capital or machines in use in a country then all such income should bear the same total tax liability which would be achieved if all countries operated an exemption double taxation relief system on a destination country basis. If, in turn, one advocates equal treatment of income from capital accruing to stockholders resident in a country then this could be achieved by an exemption double taxation relief system on a origin country basis. It may be noted that a credit double taxation relief system embodies

---

6.4 It is also counter to the traditional concerns of equity to apply these notions to companies rather than persons. Most economists would regard companies for the purpose of equity discussions as of secondary importance to the persons who have claims (equity and bond claims) on the company.

neither of these principles of horizontal equity and is difficult to justify on such grounds.

The UK tax authorities seem to have adopted the view that they are concerned with relieving double taxation[5] of corporate profits and on equity grounds income received from abroad should not be placed in an advantageous tax position relative to profits accruing to a domestic company. This could happen (in their eyes) if an exemption system of double tax relief were to operate. The fact that a British based multinational enterprise may end up paying more tax than if it had generated the same profits as a domestic company is viewed as a result of the operation of foreign tax systems and is a matter outside the jurisdiction of UK tax authorities.

Equity aspects of double tax relief for multinational enterprises can also be examined from the benefit and ability to pay approaches often suggested in the public finance literature.[6] It is often argued that it is difficult to justify any of the corporate tax structures operating in advanced economies solely on a benefit approach if benefits solely accruing to corporations are considered. The majority of benefits financed by any tax system in all probability accrue to individuals rather than companies[7] and so a benefit-related approach would typically produce low tax rates on multinational subsidiaries in origin countries as the foreign stockholders receive few of the benefits financed by the origin country tax system. With an ability to pay approach difficulties are raised by the question is it the ability of the company or the ultimate stockholders that is at issue, and if the latter their ability vis à vis whom?

When one turns from problems of equity to those of stabilisation the issues involved with double taxation relief for multinational enterprises

---

6.5 It is important to note, however, that the view is not taken that all double taxation of any form within the tax system should be relieved. Thus, double taxation of consumption expenditures exists through value added tax combined with excise taxes on expenditures; the double taxation of corporate profits through corporation tax and personal income tax still exists; and so on.

6.6 See, for instance, *International tax differentials for multinational corporations: equity and efficiency considerations*, Peggy B. Musgrave, a report prepared for the UN conference on multinational corporations, 1 June 1973 and R.A. and P.B. Musgrave 'Inter-nation Equity' in *Modern Fiscal Issues: Essays in honour of Carl S. Shoup* (ed.) R.M. Bird and J.G. Head, 1972.

6.7 Imputing benefits of public sector activity to economic agents (persons and companies) is a statistical exercise that some would regard as dangerous and this statement is to be treated with an (intended) degree of caution. Even if one accepts the description of the position on imputation of public sector benefits, one can still counter the argument made by pointing to the much smaller share of taxes paid by companies rather than persons.

are of importance, but in quantitative terms (usually) of a secondary order of magnitude in comparison with other taxation issues. Taxes of all forms fulfil a stabilisation role within any economic system and the tax treatment of multinational enterprises can be of importance for the balance of payments. Flows of capital income across national borders can be substantial for advanced economies,[8] and the taxation of these flows of importance for the balance of payments. Stabilisation policy may thus in some circumstances dictate that a special tax rate be applied to income of multinational companies although no such justification appears to have dictated policy to date in any of the major developed economies.

D Separate accounting v. formula apportionment

The previous two sections of this chapter have looked at justifications for systems of double taxation relief for multinational enterprises. While one can find justifications one can also query the wisdom of tax arrangements which give rise to the double taxation problem in the first place. The systems of taxation of multinational enterprises presented here, as has been seen, rely very heavily on a principle which may be termed 'separate accounting'.[9]

A multinational enterprise may be thought of as a single economic entity whose operations happen to straddle two or more countries. By requiring such an enterprise to negotiate separately with a number of tax authorities a requirement is placed on such a company to produce separate accounts on a territorial basis; a requirement which is not made on a domestic company. This is the principle of separate accounting. The requirement, of course, raises all sorts of problems as to the composition of such accounts. The allocation on a territorial basis of know-how, development costs, and a whole range of costs connected with central administration must inevitably be somewhat arbitrary.

6.8 The UK national accounts report a figure of £4,271 million for property income from abroad for 1973 and £1,784 million for property income due abroad out of a GNP at factor cost of £63,271 million; some of this will, however, involve persons rather than companies. (See *National Income and Expenditure 1963–1973* p. 11, HMSO.)

6.9 See *Taxation of inter-state and multinational corporations* Charles E. McLure Jr; a report prepared for the United Nations Conference on Multinational Corporation, 1 June 1973. This section relies heavily on McLure's presentation of these issues as they are treated in the US state-wide corporation tax structures.

An alternative to this set of procedures is the so-called 'formula apportionment' approach: the system adopted for the double taxation questions which arise due to the operation of state-wide corporate taxes in the USA. Rather than attempt to decide how much of a company's profits originates within a particular geographical region, the state tax authorities attempt to decide how much of the nation-wide corporate profit (i.e. the national tax base) shall be deemed to have arisen in that particular state. This usually involves the application of some formula (hence formula apportionment) which typically takes a fraction of national sales, property and pay-roll which are located in the state. Such a procedure avoids exempting income taxed elsewhere or crediting corporations for taxes paid elsewhere as the tax base which is allocated is unaffected by dividend flows between affiliated companies.

While the avoidance of direct double taxation problems is clearly a great benefit from this approach, there are a number of new problems which in turn are raised. The tax authorities must be reasonably consistent one with another so that they do not finish up in total levying tax on an excess of the true tax base. The state-wide problems in the US are eased considerably by the existence of a federal government which can, at least in principle, impose a degree of uniformity between the states and can also provide the national tax base to be divided. A corresponding international agency to mediate between nations would be needed were such an approach to be attempted in the case of the international taxation of multinational enterprises. While a world-wide agency might be impossible in the forseeable future, an agency within the EEC involved in the apportioning of the profits of EEC based corporations might possibly go some way towards easing the harmonisation problems within the EEC and would seem worthy of consideration. A final point on formula apportionment to be borne in mind is that the apportionment itself still bears features of the requirement of separate accounting. Whatever formula is applied some arbitration will be necessary as for instance, which sales are located where,[10] and even whether a company operates in a particular locality.

E   Tax deferral and its importance

A final point in the discussion of taxation of multinational enterprises in this chapter is that the existence of tax deferral opportunities can

---

6.10 Mail order business can be a problem, for instance.

substantially alter the appropriate form and extent of double taxation relief when viewed from the standpoint of national interest.

The term 'deferral privilege' refers to the fact that multinational enterprises (both typically and effectively) incur no tax liability in the destination country until profits are actually remitted. This feature would be of little importance were it not for the fact that tax rates across different countries typically differ by substantial amounts. This is particularly pronounced in the case of tax havens – those jurisdictions with zero or extremely low tax rates. These areas, of course, are attractive due to the differences in tax rates between themselves and the advanced market economies and so offer tax haven advantages of deferral to profits *en route* to parent multinational companies located in countries operating credit systems of double taxation relief.[11] In periods of substantial inflation and high interest rates, deferral of tax even for only a few years substantially reduces the effective tax incurred on the whole undertaking.

It is clearly difficult to put any precise numbers on the magnitudes involved, although Musgrave[12] has recently estimated that subsidiaries of US parents in 1970 paid $0.9 billion less in foreign profits taxes than they would have paid under US tax rates had they remitted all profits. Out of before-tax profits from US direct investments abroad of about $17.5 billion in 1970, this tax saving is not insubstantial. The US position is, however, somewhat complicated and may not represent a fair comparison for other economies in this regard, but the general point that the existence of the deferral privilege may affect the appropriate tax policy towards multinational enterprise is still worth emphasising.

6.11 Tax havens may also be useful as vehicles for the earnings in one foreign country to be restaged in another without the need to pass through the home country.
6.12 P.B. Musgrave 'Tax preferences to Foreign Investment' in *The Economics of Federal Subsidy Programs* Joint Economic Committee of the US Congress.

7. The taxation of income passing through two or more companies resident in different countries

We shall now discuss in more detail certain double taxation problems which are peculiar to groups of companies which have member companies resident in different countries. In chapter 4 we considered in outline the position of a parent company resident in one country which has a trading subsidiary resident in another country, and we observed that if the subsidiary paid a dividend out of its trading profits to the parent company, which in turn distributed that dividend to its shareholders, there would be four charges to tax on that income flow in the absence of any double taxation relief.[1] In domestic cases excessive taxation of inter-corporate dividend flows is often relieved by provisions like the UK group income and franked investment income provisions.

A Where the destination country has an exemption system of double taxation relief

Where the typical exemption arrangements exist the position will be as follows. The trading profits of the subsidiary company will be subjected to corporation tax in the origin country. When the subsidiary pays the dividend to its parent, the amount of withholding tax which the origin country can levy on that dividend will be limited to a figure fixed by the double tax treaty between the two countries.[2] The dividend received by the parent company will be exempt from corporate tax in the destination

---

7.1 See the example on pages 42 and 43.
7.2 Usually the maximum permitted withholding tax will be between 10% and 15% of the dividend.

country because it has an exemption system. When the parent company distributes that dividend to its shareholders they will be liable to personal income tax on that dividend. The exemption system does not, however, entirely solve the problem. The income flow suffered a dividend withholding tax in the origin country and the shareholders were subjected to full personal income tax on the dividend they received in the destination country without any relief in respect of the source country withholding tax. On the hypotheses to which the authors subscribe this constitutes an element of unrelieved international double taxation.

Example 1. Company A, resident in state I, owns a subsidiary, company B, which is resident in state II. The shareholders in company A are all resident in state I. Both states have a classical system of corporation tax with a rate of 50% and both states have a basic rate of personal income tax of 30%. Under the Double Tax Treaty between the two states dividend withholding tax is limited to 15% and there is an exemption system of double tax relief.

On a profit of 100 company B will pay state II corporation tax of 50 and if it distributes the balance of 50 to company A that dividend will suffer state II withholding tax of 7.5 leaving a net dividend of 42.5. The net dividend of 42.5 received by company A will be exempt from state I corporation tax in company A's hands. When company A distributes to its shareholders the 42.5 which it has received, they will be liable to basic rate income tax at 30% on that 42.5 which is 12.75, leaving them with a net amount of 29.75. In a purely domestic state I or state II case the shareholders could receive a net dividend of 35 out of a profit of 100 accruing to the company[3] which is 5.25 more than the 29.75 received by the shareholders in our example.

B   Where the destination country has a credit system of double taxation relief

1   *The position in principle*

Where a credit system is in operation the problem is more complex. In that case the dividend received by the parent company will not be

---

7.3 The calculation would be as follows: on a profit of 100 the company would pay corporation tax of 50 and when it distributed the remaining 50, the shareholders would bear tax at 30% on the 50 (= 15) leaving a net dividend of 35.

exempt from corporation tax in the destination country; instead the parent company will be allowed a credit for the origin country tax. The question is, for what origin country tax is the parent company given a credit? If the credit were confined to the dividend withholding tax exacted by the source country the credit would be small and there would be a considerable amount of international double taxation unrelieved.[4] Accordingly some countries which operate a credit system[5] give the parent a credit not only for the origin country withholding tax but also for the origin country corporation tax suffered by the subsidiary company. This is known as relief for underlying tax and it will now be more fully explored.

2 Relief for underlying tax

The simplest case involving relief for underlying tax is where only two companies and only two countries are involved. The problem of underlying tax becomes even more complex where there are third and fourth tier companies and three or more countries involved.

a Cases involving only two countries. The notion of underlying tax can most conveniently be illustrated by the following example:

Example 2. (i) *Facts* Company A is resident in state I and owns all the shares in a subsidiary, company B, which is resident in state II. State II has a classical system of corporation tax with a rate of corporation tax of 50% and a basic rate of tax of 30% on dividends. That basic rate of 30% is required to be withheld by the company paying the dividend and that company must pay to the fiscal authorities the amount of tax withheld. State I also has a classical system of corporation tax with a tax rate of 50%. The double taxation treaty between state I and state II provides that there shall be a credit system of double tax relief between the two states and that withholding taxes on dividends in that country where the paying company is located shall be limited to 15%.

(ii) *Tax liability in the absence of relief for underlying tax* If the double tax arrangements made no further provision, the position would be as follows. On a profit of 100 company B would pay state II tax of 50. If company B paid the remaining 50 to company A by way of dividend, company B would have to withhold tax of 7.5[6] on that dividend, and

---

7.4 On the authors' hypotheses, see chapter 2 and chapter 4.
7.5 e.g. the UK.
7.6 The withholding tax is 15% (the maximum permitted by the Double Tax Treaty) of the dividend of 50=7.5.

account to the state II fiscal authorities for that withholding tax. The gross dividend of 50 would be liable to state I corporation tax in company A's hands, and therefore company A would be liable to state I tax of 50% of $50 = 25$, less any credit in respect of foreign tax. The only state II tax which has been charged on the *dividend* is the withholding tax of 7.5 and therefore company A's state I tax would be $25 - 7.5 = 17.5$. Under such a system of double taxation company A would get no credit for the corporation tax suffered by company B in state II on the technical ground that this was not tax levied on the dividend.

(iii) *Tax liability where relief for underlying tax is given by state I* To reduce the burden of tax which would otherwise be suffered, credit systems of double taxation often provide relief for the underlying tax suffered on profits out of which the dividend was paid. The relief is usually confined to underlying taxes of the same type as income tax and corporation tax. Thus relief for underlying tax is not given for taxes on wealth, social security taxes, payroll taxes and property taxes. The usual method is to take the net dividend received by company A and gross it up by reference to all the foreign tax suffered which is eligible for underlying relief, work out the state I tax on that gross amount, and then grant company A a credit in respect of all the foreign tax which is eligible for relief. Thus the dividend received by company A, grossed-up by reference to all the state II tax,[7] amounts to 100, state I tax on that is 50, less the credit for the state II tax of 50 (underlying corporation tax) + 7.5 (dividend withholding tax) = 57.5. The state I tax is therefore nil. This example thus illustrates the method of calculating relief for underlying tax; that is to gross up income receipts in the destination country by all taxes paid in the origin country (which are eligible for relief) whether or not those taxes were technically paid from the income defined as crossing the border.

b Cases involving three or more countries. In the above example the income flow involved has only passed through two countries. If, however the income has passed through three or more countries, the question arises whether the country of final destination will give relief for all the underlying tax paid in each of the three or more countries through which the income flow has passed. Let us suppose that in example 1 the trade were carried on in state III by company C which is a subsidiary of company B, and company C pays dividends out of its trading profits to company B which in turn pays a dividend to company

---

7.7 i.e. state II corporation tax charged on company B's profits and the state II withholding tax levied on the dividend.

A. In determining what tax credit is to be given to company A, the government of state I will have to decide whether to confine the tax credit to the underlying tax suffered in state II or whether to extend it to the underlying tax suffered in state III as well. Some systems of taxation (for example the UK) allow a tax credit for all underlying tax no matter how many companies and countries the dividend has passed through.[8] The US system does not allow relief for underlying tax suffered by companies beyond third tier companies.

c The extent to which relief for underlying tax cures the difficulty. The credit system even if it gives a credit for underlying tax does not entirely eliminate the basic problem, because it does not carry the relief for the origin country withholding tax and underlying tax through to the shareholders in the parent company. Accordingly this system also may result in a multinational enterprise being subjected to a greater total tax liability than purely domestic enterprises of either country. In example 2 above the net amount received by the shareholders in company A will be 29.75 as compared with 35 in the case of purely domestic enterprises of either state.

C   Conclusions

Neither the credit nor the exemption systems outlined above carry the relief through to the shareholders in the destination country. This, therefore, according to the authors' hypotheses leaves an element of unrelieved international double taxation which could only be relieved by modification of the credit and exemption systems of double taxation relief.

The EEC Draft Directive on Harmonization of Company Taxation and withholding Taxes on Dividends[9] contains provisions designed to deal with this problem in respect of dividend flows within the EEC.

There is a further respect in which multinational enterprises may suffer an undue burden on dividend flows across national boundaries. Countries generally fix their corporate tax rates in the light of the rates of personal income tax on dividends. One country may adopt the policy of a lower rate of corporation tax and a higher rate of personal income tax whereas another country may adopt the opposite policy. A multinational enterprise could find its dividend flows suffering the worst of both worlds.

7.8 Provided that the recipient company controls the necessary 10% of the voting power in the paying company, see TA 1970 section 498 (4).
7.9 Discussed in chapter 13.

8. The OECD model treaty

The Organization for Economic Co-operation and Development has published a Draft Convention for the Avoidance of Double Taxation with respect to Taxes on Income and Capital. This is designed as a model form of bilateral treaty to be used by developed countries in negotiating tax treaties. It is now proposed to examine the principal provisions in this model treaty which deal with the problems outlined earlier. This examination is considered to be justified on two grounds: first because the OECD model is used as a basis for negotiation, and secondly because it provides illustrations of ways in which double taxation problems may be dealt with. The discussion in this chapter assumes throughout that all the states mentioned have adopted double tax arrangements in the form of the OECD model. Article 23 of that model treaty provides for either an exemption or a credit method for relieving double taxation and in each case it will be indicated which alternative the states concerned are thought to have adopted.

A Relief of double taxation which would arise by reason of dual residence

Double taxation could often occur because a company was treated by the tax code of state I as resident in state I and by the tax code of state II as resident in state II. The OECD model treaty contains provisions dealing with this problem.

Article 4 deals with 'residence' for the purposes of the treaty. Article 4.1 provides that the term 'resident of a contracting state' means any person who under the law of that state, is liable to taxation therein by reason of this 'domicile, residence, place of management or any other criterion of a similar nature'. If applying article 4.1 produces dual residence, recourse must be had to articles 4.2¹ and 4.3 which contain provisions designed to eliminate that dual residence. Article 4.3 provides that, if applying article 4.1, a company² is a resident of both contracting states, then 'it shall be deemed to be a resident of the contracting state in which its place of effective management is situated'.

B Relief of double taxation which would arise because the taxpayer was resident in one country and the source was situated in another country

1 Treatment of the business profits of companies trading through branches

Article 7 of the model treaty provides that where a resident of one state carries on business in another state, the profit of that business shall be taxable only in the state of residence, unless the person carrying on the business has a 'permanent establishment' in the other state.

Permanent establishment is defined in article 5. Article 5.1 contains a general definition of a permanent establishment, namely, 'a fixed place of business in which the business of the enterprise is wholly or partly carried on', and the remaining paragraphs of article 5 contain detailed provisions prescribing that certain things shall and certain things shall not constitute permanent establishments.

Where a resident of one state carries on business in another state through a permanent establishment, article 7 provides that the state where the permanent establishment is situated can tax the business profit attributable to that permanent establishment. If company A resident in state I carries on business in state II through a branch, and under the domestic systems of tax in states I and II the business profits of that branch are taxable in both state I and state II, the model treaty would have the following effect. Article 7 would not relieve the double taxation. Under article 7 state I is permitted to tax company A's business profits on the ground of residence. The branch in state II would constitute a permanent establishment within the meaning of article 5³ and therefore by virtue of article 7 state II would be permitted to tax the profit attributable to that branch.

8.1 Article 4.2 deals with individuals and therefore does not merit further consideration in this work.
8.2 Or other person not being an individual.
8.3 See article 5.2 (b).

To relieve the double taxation, recourse must be had to article 23. If these two states have adopted the exemption provisions in article 23A, then the profit of this branch will be taxable in state II, but exempt in state I.[4] If the two states have adopted the credit provisions in article 23B, then the branch profits will be liable to tax in state II, and the state II tax will be a credit against company A's liability to tax in state I in respect of those profits.

2 Treatment of companies carrying on trades through subsidiaries

Suppose company A, resident in state I, owns all the shares in company B which is resident and carries on business in state II and the domestic tax systems of each state provide that tax shall be levied in that state if either the taxpayer is resident there or the source of the income is situated there.

a Treatment of compc 1y B's business profits. Company B's business profit will be taxable in state II on the grounds that the company is resident there.[5]

Company A will not be liable to tax in either state on those business profits because company A is not carrying on the business.

b Treatment of dividends paid by company B out of its business profit. If there were no double tax arrangements in force in either state, such a dividend would be taxable in state II on the ground that the source of the dividend, namely the shares, was situated in that state and it would also be taxable in state I because company A, the recipient of the dividend, is resident in that state.

Article 10.1 provides that the dividends may be taxed in state I. Article 10.2 provides that the dividend may also be taxed in state II, but the amount of state II tax is limited to 5% on the gross amount of the dividend if the recipient company owns directly at least 25% of the shares in the paying company, and to 15% on the gross amount of the dividend in all other cases. Here, as company B is a wholly owned subsidiary of company A, the rate of state II tax is limited to 5%.

If the two states have adopted the credit provisions, then the state II tax on the dividend is allowed as a credit against company A's liability to corporation tax in state I on that dividend.[6]

8.4 See article 23A.1.
8.5 See article 7.
8.6 See article 23B 1 (a).

If the two states have adopted the exemption provisions in article 23A, then the result is the same, because article 23A contains special provisions dealing with interest and dividends. Article 23A.1 usually has the effect that the income concerned is exempt from tax in the country of origin, but the operation of Article 23A.1 is stated to be 'subject to the provisions of paragraph 2'. Article 23A.2 provides that where income is liable to tax in both states under article 10[7] or article 11,[8] then the tax levied in the country of origin shall be allowed as a credit against the tax in the country of destination. The reason for this special provision in article 23A.2 is that in the case of dividends and interest articles 10 and 11 are designed to divide the tax between the two states and therefore an exemption method of relieving double tax is inappropriate because it would defeat that objective. In neither case does the model treaty provide relief for underlying tax.

Article 10 paragraphs 1 and 2 do not apply where article 10 paragraph 4 applies. Article 10.4 provides that if the recipient company has a permanent establishment in the country where the paying company is resident and the recipient company's shareholding is 'effectively connected' with that permanent establishment then 10.1 and 2 do not apply and article 7 does. Thus if company A has a permanent establishment in state II and company A's shareholding in company B is effectively connected with that permanent establishment, article 7 will apply with the result that the dividend will be subjected to full taxation in both states.

3   Treatment of interest

If company A resident in state I lends money at a commercial rate of interest to company B resident in state II, the tax treatment of that interest is as follows. Article 11 paragraphs 1 and 2 provide that state I and state II may tax this interest, but state II tax shall be limited to 10%. It is provided, however, that if the recipient has a permanent establishment in the state in which the interest arises and the debt claim from which the interest arises is effectively connected with that permanent establishment, article 11 paragraphs 1 and 2 shall not apply, but article 7 shall apply instead.[9]

Thus where company A does not have a permanent establishment in state II the interest will be taxed in state II at a rate not exceeding 10%.

8.7 Article 10 deals with dividends.
8.8 Article 11 deals with interest.
8.9 See article 11.4.

The state II tax will be allowed as a credit against company A's liability to corporation tax in state I. This is so whether article 23A or 23B is adopted. If article 23B (credit method) is adopted, the 10% tax on the interest levied by state II will be allowed as a credit against state I tax. If article 23A (exemption method) is adopted, the same result will ensue because article 23A.2 will apply. Under article 23A.2 the interest will be subjected to the 10% tax in state II and will be taxable in state I subject to a credit for the state II tax.[10]

It will not make any difference if company B is a subsidiary of company A, because it is expressly provided that a subsidiary is not a 'permanent establishment'.[11]

Where owing to a special relationship between the payer and the payee the interest payment is in excess of a commercial rate, article 11, paragraphs 1 and 2 apply to the interest up to the commercial rate and not to the excess.[12]

4 Treatment of royalties

Royalties are taxable in the state where the recipient resides and are exempt from tax in the state of origin,[13] except where the recipient has a permanent establishment in the state of origin and the right or property giving rise to the royalties is effectively connected with that permanent establishment in which case article 7 applies.[14] Payment of royalties in excess of a commercial rate by reason of a special relationship between the payer and payee, are treated in the same way as excessive interest payments.[15] Thus if company B, resident in state II, pays royalties at a normal commercial rate to company A, resident in state I, and company A has no permanent establishment in state II, the royalties will be taxed in state I, but exempt from tax in state II. If, however, company A has a branch in state II and the royalties are payable under a licence agreement in respect of a patented invention developed by that branch, then the royalty provisions in article 12 will not apply and the royalty payments will be governed by article 7. Under article 7 the royalty payments will be taxable in state II because company A has a permanent establishment there and is taxable in state I because company A is resident there. The resulting double taxation will then be dealt with by article 23. If article

---

8.10 See the preceding discussion of this in connection with dividends.
8.11 See article 5.6
8.12 See article 11.6.
8.13 See article 12.1
8.14 See article 12.3
8.15 See article 12.4

23A has been adopted the royalty payments will be exempt from tax in state II, whereas if article 23B has been adopted the royalty payments will be taxed in state II and then the State II tax will be a credit against the state I tax. It is thus in the case where the credit provisions in article 23B have been adopted that it makes a vital difference whether the royalties are within article 12 or article 7.

5   *Treatment of payments for the supply of goods or services*

These payments will normally be deductible as a business expense in computing the profits of the paying company. The payments will have to be entered as a receipt in computing the business profits of the recipient company and the taxation of those business profits will be governed by articles 7 and 23.

Article 9 deals with transfer pricing, i.e. attempts to cause profits to arise in one country rather than another by artificial prices charged by a company in one country for goods or services provided by an associated company in another country.

Under article 9, where conditions are made or imposed between two associated[16] enterprises[17] in their commercial and financial relations which differ from those which would be made between independent enterprises, any profits which, but for those conditions, would have accrued to one of the enterprises may be included in the profits of that enterprise and taxed accordingly. Where the price is too low, tax avoidance is nullified by the state which taxes the business profit of the recipient company deeming that company to have received the full arm's length price and requiring it to enter that deemed receipt in its profit and loss account. This may result in an element of double taxation, because the paying company may be able to deduct only the actual price paid in computing its profits.

Where the price is excessive, tax avoidance can be nullified by the state which taxes the business profits of the paying company, permitting that company to deduct only the arm's length price when computing its business profits for tax purposes. Again there will be an element of double taxation because the recipient company will be required to enter the actual price paid in its profit and loss account. Many feel that this double taxation is richly deserved by those who seek to secure a saving of tax by adjusting inter-corporate prices in this way. This may well be so, but some multinational companies complain that they may be

---

8.16 'Associated' enterprise is defined in article 9(a) and (b).
8.17 'Enterprise' is defined in article 3.1 (d).

prejudiced by such anti-avoidance provisions when they are not attempting any tax avoidance. They argue that it is often very difficult to determine what is an arm's length price for certain types of goods and services,[18] and they may find that one fiscal authority takes a different view from another as to what is the arm's length price for particular goods or services. This problem of transfer pricing is examined in more detail in chapter 15.

C The effect of different systems of corporation tax on limitation of withholding taxes on dividends

As has already been explained, article 10 of the OECD model treaty suggests 15% as a maximum rate of tax which may be levied by the state in which the paying company is resident. In practice states quite often agree to a maximum withholding tax on dividends of about that figure.

If one looks only at the amount of withholding tax which the fiscal authorities in the origin country will be able to exact from the dividend, then the loss of revenue caused by the limitation on the withholding tax imposed by the double tax arrangements, will be the same whether that country has a classical, two-rate or imputation system of corporate tax. If however, one looks at the total tax levied (comprising both underlying corporation tax and dividend withholding tax), the loss of total revenue of the income flow varies according to which system of corporation tax operates in the origin country. This hypothesis will now be considered in more detail with the aid of the examples. In each example the rates of tax have been selected so that the total burden of tax on distributed profits in a purely domestic case would be 50%. Each example postulates maximum distributions and no reserves out of which the company can pay its tax.

A country which has a classical system with a withholding tax of more than 15% in domestic cases will suffer a loss of revenue on dividends flowing abroad because of the reduction of the withholding tax to 15%, but at least it will have exacted its full rate of corporation tax on the profit out of which the dividend is paid.[19]

Example 1. Company A is resident in state I which has a classical system of corporation tax with a corporate tax rate of 40% and a

---

8.18 e.g. a half made article or a patented drug.
8.19 Unless that profit is composed of foreign source income in respect of which double tax relief is available to the company paying the dividend.

withholding tax of 16.67% in domestic cases. In a domestic case the tax on a profit of 100 will be as follows: 40 corporation tax, plus withholding tax at 16.67% on the gross dividend of 60 = 10, making a total burden of 50. In a case where the whole dividend is distributed to foreign shareholders the withholding tax on the dividend will be 15% of 60 = 9. Thus the loss of total revenue is 1.

A country which operates a two-rate system suffers a greater loss of total revenue, because under its two rate system distributed profits will have been taxed at a lower rate and yet it will not be able to exact more than 15% withholding tax on distributions abroad.

Example 2. Company A is resident in state II which has a two-rate system of corporation tax with a rate of 50% on undistributed profits and 20% on distributed profits with a withholding tax of 30% on distributions. In a purely domestic case on a profit of 100 there would be corporation tax of 28.57 and the gross dividend of 71.43 would be taxed at 30% = 21.43, a total burden of 28.57 + 21.43 = 50.

In a case where the whole dividend is distributed to foreign shareholders the rate of withholding tax would be reduced to 15%. There would be corporation tax of 28.57 plus withholding tax of 15% of 71.43 = 39.29. The loss on total revenue suffered by state II is 50 − 39.29 = 10.71.

A country operating an imputation system will charge the profits of the company to corporation tax in the usual way. It will then impute part of that corporation tax to domestic shareholders by way of a tax credit. It can then deny a tax credit to foreign shareholders without infringing treaty provisions relating to maximum rates of withholding tax on dividends because the tax it has exacted is corporation tax levied on the company, not a tax on dividends.

Example 3. Company A is resident in state III which has an imputation system of corporation tax with a corporate tax rate of 50% with a tax credit of 3/5ths of the net dividend which exactly covers the domestic shareholders' liability to personal income tax. In a purely domestic case the total revenue on a profit of 100 will be simply 50% corporation tax. In a case where the dividends are paid to foreign shareholders, state III can deny them a tax credit so that they cannot claim a refund. The result is that state III's total revenue is undiminished.

There is a school of thought based upon these assumptions, that an imputation system is preferable to a two-rate system when it comes to negotiation of double tax treaties. The reasoning being that a country with a two-rate system would wish to negotiate a high withholding tax on dividends flowing abroad to reduce the loss of total revenue, whereas a country having an imputation system would be unconcerned about the maximum dividend withholding tax and would therefore hope to negotiate from a position of strength. This was the principal reason why the Select Committee on Corporation Tax recommended Parliament to adopt an imputation rather than a two-rate system for the UK.[20] It may well be, however, that the other country negotiating a new double tax treaty will be in a position to put pressure on the country having the imputation system to give up some of its revenue.

In the recent negotiations concerning the new USA/UK Double Tax Treaty, the USA authorities have succeeded in persuading the UK authorities to allow US resident shareholders a tax credit in respect of half the normal UK imputation.[21]

8.20 See Cmd. No. 622 1971 – Committee Report paragraphs 23–6 and the evidence of Mr J.F. Chown (Minutes of Evidence, paragraphs 244–82).
8.21 Subject to some UK withholding tax, see chapter 10.

9. Relief from international double taxation in the UK

The UK has a network of bilateral treaties providing double taxation relief and in addition there are some provisions in the UK tax code which provide for unilateral relief.[1] It is not feasible in a work of this size to provide a detailed commentary upon all these treaties and therefore the authors have selected the UK/Belgian Double Tax Treaty[2] for more detailed consideration to serve as a fairly recent example of the type of arrangements which are often made. In addition reference will be made to other UK treaties by way of contrast or further amplification and an outline of the unilateral relief will be given. Part of chapter 10 will be devoted to a consideration of the provisions relating to dividends contained in the new UK/US Double tax Treaty, the text of which was agreed upon in 1975, because those provisions differ considerably from the ones usually contained in treaties to which the UK is party.

A Treaty relief

As we have seen in earlier chapters, double taxation arises where the same profit[3] is liable to tax in two or more countries at the same time.

Treaties to which UK is party deal with this in one or more of the following ways:–

i The treaty may contain provisions designed to prevent double taxation arising by reason of dual residence.

9.1 See TA 1970, section 498.
9.2 The Double Taxation Relief (Taxes on Income) (Belgium) Order 1970 (SI 1970 No. 636).
9.3 The authors would reiterate that their hypothesis is that for these purposes a company's income and any distribution which it makes out of that income to its shareholders is one profit.

ii The treaty provides in some cases that the profit shall be taxed in only one of the countries concerned.[4]

iii The treaty may provide that although the profit may be taxed in both countries, the tax which may be levied by the origin country shall be limited to a rate which is lower than the one which would otherwise be exigible[5] and that in taxing the profit the destination country shall give a credit for the tax suffered in the origin country.[6]

iv The treaty may permit full taxation of the profit in the origin country and provide that the profit shall also be taxable in the destination country, but subject to a credit for the tax levied in the origin country.[7]

It is now proposed to consider the relief from double taxation which is provided by the UK/Belgian treaty for various situations and types of income.

1 Dual residence

Article IV of the UK/Belgian treaty deals with the problem of dual residence and the provisions relating to companies are as follows:

'(1) For the purposes of this Convention, the term "resident of one of the territories" means any person who, under the law of that territory, is liable to taxation therein by reason of his domicile, residence, place of management or any other criterion of a similar nature and includes in the case of Belgium any person liable to tax there by reference to the aggregate amount of his income produced or received in Belgium.

(3) Where by reason of the provisions of paragraph (1) a person other than an individual is a resident of both territories, then it shall be

---

9.4 e.g. Article XII (1) of the UK/Belgian Treaty which (subject to article XII (3) provides that royalties shall be taxed only in the country where the recipient is resident (i.e. an exemption on an origin basis).

9.5 e.g. ibid. Article XI of which paragraph (1) permits taxation of interest in the destination country and paragraph (2) (subject to paragraphs (4) and (5)) limits the origin country tax on interest to a maximum of 15%.

9.6 Where the UK is the destination country the credit is provided for by article XXIII (1) and where Belgium is the destination country by article XXIII (2) (a) (ii).

9.7 e.g. Where a UK resident company has a branch in Belgium profits of that branch will be liable to full tax in Belgium (see article VII (1) and the profits of the branch will form part of the UK company's profits for corporation tax purposes (see TA 1970). Section 243 (1); under article XXIII (1) the Belgian tax charged on the branch profits will be a credit against UK corporation tax on those profits.

deemed to be a resident of the territory in which its place of effective management is situated.'

2 Business Profits

Article VII deals with these as follows:
'(1) The profits of an enterprise of one of the territories shall be taxable only in that territory unless the enterprise carries on business in the other territory through a permanent establishment situated therein. If the enterprise carries on business as aforesaid, the profits of the enterprise may be taxed in the other territory but only so much of them as is attributable to that permanent establishment.' Thus business profits may always be taxed in the country where the person[8] carrying on the trade resides, but will not be taxed in the country where the trade is carried on unless the person carrying on the trade has a permanent establishment there. If the person carrying on the trade has a permanent establishment in the origin country, the profits of that permanent establishment may also be taxed by the origin country. If the UK is the destination country the taxpayer's trading profits (including the profits from the Belgian permanent establishment) will be liable to UK tax, subject to a credit for the Belgian origin country tax. If Belgium is the destination country the profits from the UK permanent establishment will be exempt from Belgian tax,[9] provided that UK tax has been paid on those profits. Article V(1) contains the general definition of 'permanent establishment', namely a fixed place of business in which the activity of the enterprise is wholly or partly carried on. The remaining paragraphs of Article V elaborate on this definition by providing that certain things shall and certain things shall not constitute a permanent establishment for the purposes of the treaty.

It should be noted that a subsidiary company does not constitute a permanent establishment of the parent because article V paragraph 7 provides: 'The fact that a company which is a resident of one of the territories controls or is controlled by a company which is a resident of the other territory, or which carries on business in that other territory (whether through a permanent establishment or otherwise), shall not of itself constitute either company a permanent establishment of the other.' The operation of article VII dealing with business profits will now be illustrated by the following examples.

9.8 Whether an individual or a company.
9.9 However under article XXIII (2)(b) (i) the income of the UK permanent establishment can be taken into account in computing the rate(s) applicable to the Belgian taxpayers other income; this is known as the system of exemption with progression which is more fully explained in chapter 10, at page 108 below.

Example 1. An individual[10] resident in Belgium, bought land in the UK with a view to selling it at a profit. The purchases and sales are to be carried out by English firms of estate agents and solicitors having authority to complete the sales without recourse to the Belgian principal. The sales will constitute trading transactions for the purposes of UK tax and since the contracts are made here the trade is 'exercised in the UK' and therefore constitutes a UK source for UK tax purposes.[11] Apart from the provisions in the treaty the profits of that trade would be liable to UK tax.[12]

The effect of article VII of the treaty is that UK tax will not be chargeable unless the Belgian has a permanent establishment in the UK. Article V, paragraph (5) provides that the UK estate agents and solicitors do not constitute a permanent establishment and therefore the trading profits are exempt from UK tax. The trading profits will be liable to tax in Belgium; the exemption from Belgian tax on foreign source income in article XXIII paragraph 2(b) (i) will not apply here because the profits have not been subjected to UK tax.

Example 2. A UK resident company carries on a trade in Belgium through a branch located there. Since that branch constitutes a permanent establishment[13] the treaty permits the Belgian tax authorities to levy tax on the branch profits and accordingly the profits of the branch will be liable to Belgian tax under the provisions of the Belgian domestic tax code.

Those branch profits will also be liable to UK tax (together with the rest of the company's profits),[14] but the Belgian tax on the branch profits will be a credit against UK corporation tax on those profits.[15] Thus on a profit of the Belgian branch of 100 Belgian tax at 48% would be charged. The profit of 100 would be liable to UK Corporation tax at 52% minus the credit of 48 in respect of the Belgian tax. Accordingly the total tax charged would be Belgian tax of 48 plus UK of 4.

9.10 An individual has been selected as the taxpayer in order to illustrate the operation of article VII without the necessity of considering whether the English estate agents and solicitors constitute an 'agency' for the purposes of TA 1970, section 246(1); if they did not and if the Belgian taxpayer were a company, UK corporation tax would not be exigible apart from any provision in the treaty, (see section 246(1)).

9.11 See TA 1970, section 108, schedule D, paragraph 1(a)(iii) and *Grainger v. Gough* (1896) AC 325; 3TC 462 (HL) *Firestone Tyre Co. Ltd v. Lewellin* (1957), WLR 464; 37 TC III (HL).

9.12 It would be a charge to income tax under schedule D case I.

9.13 See article V, paragraph 2(b).

9.14 See TA 1970, section 246 (1).

9.15 See article XXIII, paragraph (1).

3 Interest

The withholding tax which the origin country may levy on interest payable to a resident of the other country is limited to 15%,[16] except where the recipient has in the origin country a permanent establishment with which debt is effectively connected in which case the interest can be taxed in full.[17]

Interest is liable to tax in the destination country[18] subject to a credit for the origin country tax.[19]

Example 3. A UK resident company receives interest from a Belgian source. There will be Belgian withholding tax of 15% which will be a credit against UK corporation tax on that interest.

4 Royalties

Royalties are exempt from tax in the origin country[20] unless the recipient has a permanent establishment in the origin country with which the property or right giving rise to the royalties is effectively connected.[21]

5 Dividends

a The UK/Belgian treaty. Article X, paragraph (2) limits the withholding tax on dividends to 15% of the gross amount of the dividends.

i Dividends flowing from the UK to Belgium. The position as regards dividends paid by the UK companies to Belgian companies is that the UK company will be liable to pay ACT in respect of that dividend, but since technically that ACT is not a tax *on dividends*, the 15% limit does not apply to it. A UK resident individual shareholder would receive a tax credit in respect of the ACT which would cover his liability to

---

9.16 See article XI, paragraph (2).
9.17 See article XI, paragraph (4).
9.18 See article XI, paragraph (1).
9.19 See article XXIII, paragraph (1) (where the UK is the destination country) and article XXIII, paragraph (2)(a)(ii) where Belgium is the destination country).
9.20 Article XII, paragraph (1). Contrast the UK/Japanese Treaty which, unusually, permits a withholding tax of 10% on royalties. (See The Double Taxation Relief (Taxes on Income) (Japan) Order 1963, (SI 1963 No. 887), article VIII.)
9.21 See UK/Belgian Treaty, article XII, paragraph (3).

personal income tax at the basic rate. A UK resident corporate shareholder would have the benefit of the group relief provisions or the franked investment income provisions. Neither of these is accorded to foreign resident shareholders.

The Belgian tax treatment of a dividend received by a Belgian company from a UK company is too complicated to be within the scope of this work.[22]

ii Dividends flowing from Belgium to the UK. Where a UK company receives a dividend from a Belgian company that dividend will be liable to UK corporation tax subject to a credit for Belgian Tax. The recipient UK company will always be entitled to a credit for the Belgian withholding tax[23] and provided that the UK company owns at least 10% of the voting power in the Belgian company, relief will also be available in respect of the underlying Belgium corporation tax.[24]

b The UK/Danish treaty[25]. In 1973 a supplementary treaty was entered into between the UK and Denmark[26] in order to modify the treatment of dividends in the light of the adoption of an imputation system by the UK. This has served as a model for provisions relating to dividends in new treaties between the UK and some other countries, but the US authorities have insisted on different provisions relating to dividends being inserted in the new UK/US treaty.

Under the 1973 UK/Danish treaty the treatment of dividends paid by a company resident in the UK to a resident of Denmark is as follows:

i Where the Danish recipient is an individual or a company which controls less than 10% of the voting power in the UK company. In this case the Danish shareholder is allowed the same credit as a UK resident individual shareholder, but subject to a UK withholding tax at 15% on the aggregate of the dividend plus the tax credit.[27]

9.22 It depends upon the complex provisions in article XXIII, paragraph 2(a)(i) combined with provisions of the Belgian Tax Code dealing with inter-corporate dividends. Readers who wish to pursue this further are referred to the clear exposition in J.F. Chown: *Taxation and multinational enterprise*, pp. 42–4.
9.23 See UK/Belgian treaty article XXIII, paragraph (1).
9.24 See pages 96 and 97 below.
9.25 The principal treaty is the Double Taxation Relief (Taxes on Income) (Denmark) Order 1950 (SI 1950 No. 1195); the new provisions dealing with dividends are contained in the Double Taxation Relief (Taxes on Income) (Denmark) Order 1973 (SI 1973 No. 1326).
9.26 Hereafter called 'the 1973 UK/Danish Treaty'
9.27 Article VII, paragraphs 1(b), 2 and 3 of the UK/Danish treaty (substituted in it by the 1973 UK/Danish treaty article 1).

Example 4. In March 1976 a UK resident company paid a net dividend of 65 to a Danish resident company which has a 5% shareholding in the UK company. ACT on that dividend is 35; the dividend plus the tax credit is 100 on which UK tax is limited to 15. The Danish company can therefore recover from the UK Revenue 20 (i.e. the difference between 15 and the ACT of 35).

ii Where the Danish recipient is a company owning 10% or more of the voting power in the UK company. The dividend will have suffered full UK ACT and no tax credit is available to the Danish company.[28]

c UK/US treaty[29]. In the case of individual US shareholders of US companies owning not more then 10% of the voting power in a UK company the position is the same as under the Danish treaty.[30] In the case of US companies owning 10% or more of the voting power the US company will be allowed half the tax credit allowed to an individual in the UK less a UK withholding tax of 5% levied on the dividend plus that tax credit.[31]

Example 5. In March 1976 a UK resident company pays a dividend of 65 to a US Corporation which owns 100% of the voting power in the UK company. ACT of 35 will have been paid by the UK company. The UK tax credit in domestic cases is 35 of which half will be 17.5. UK withholding tax at 5% will be charged on the dividend of 65 plus the half credit of 17.5; and UK withholding tax will therefore be 4.13 and the US corporation will be able to recover 30.87 (i.e. the difference between the ACT of 35 and the permitted withholding tax of 4.13).

6 Inter-corporate prices

Provisions are often inserted in treaties entitling the fiscal authorities to adjust inter-corporate prices between associated companies in order to prevent transfer pricing.

Article IX of the UK/Belgium treaty permits the fiscal authorities to make such adjustments. Under the UK system the adjustment

---

9.28 See ibid. Article VII, paragraph 3.
9.29 Double Taxation Relief (Taxes on Income) (United States of America) Order 1976 SI 1976.
9.30 See UK/US treaty article 10, paragraph (2)(a)(ii).
9.31 i.e. half the credit allowed to UK individuals. See UK/US treaty article 10, paragraph (2)(a)(i).

provisions are contained in the UK tax code.[32] The broad effect of these provisions is that if a UK company sells goods or provides services for a foreign associated company at a price lower than the arm's length price the UK Revenue can tax that company on the profit it would have made if the arm's length price had been charged and if a UK company purchases goods or services from a foreign associated company at a price higher than the arm's length price, then the UK Revenue can disallow any deduction in respect of the excess expenditure in computing the UK company's profits.

7   Relief for underlying tax

Under the UK/Belgian Treaty where dividends are received by a UK company from a Belgian company in which it holds at least 10% of the voting power credit is given for underlying Belgian corporation tax as well as the withholding tax levied on the dividend.[33] The calculation of the relief for the underlying tax follows the familiar form.[34] UK corporation tax is calculated upon the dividend grossed up by reference to the Belgian tax (i.e. the withholding tax plus the Belgian underlying tax) and then a credit is given for the Belgian tax against that UK corporation tax.[35] This extends to second-tier and subsequent-tier companies provided that the UK company has indirect voting power of at least 10% in the company which has suffered the underlying corporation tax in respect of which relief is claimed.

A parent company may seek to avoid or defer its liability to tax on profits of its foreign enterprises, by causing the profits to arise in a foreign subsidiary located in a tax haven or a country which, although not a tax haven, has lower tax rates than the destination country and not repatriating those profits to the destination country. It may be asked how, at the end of the day, are the profits enjoyed? The answer is that they may be turned into capital by means of a sale of the shares in the subsidiary or a liquidation of the subsidiary or the profits may be accumulated in the subsidiary for a period of years and re-invested. This deferral of destination country tax liability permits sufficient profit to be accumulated to enable the parent to discharge the destination country

---

9.32 TA 1970, section 485. It is submitted that the treaty provision merely confirms that the UK Revenue may invoke section 485 in its dealings with enterprises of the other contracting state.
9.33 See article XXIII, paragraph 1.
9.34 The method is that prescribed in TA 1970, section 506.
9.35 For an example showing computation of relief for underlying tax, see chapter 7.

tax when the profit is finally repatriated and leave a substantial net receipt. Under UK law there are the following provisions which may be used to combat this:

a Exchange control permission may be required before funds can be invested in the subsidiary and repatriation of a proportion of the subsidiary's profits may be made a condition of the grant of exchange control permission.

b It may not be possible to set up the subsidiary without the consent of the Treasury under section 482 of the TA 1970[36] and repatriation of profits may be made a condition of such permission.

c Section 485 of the TA 1970 may be invoked to prevent the parent causing profits to arise in the foreign subsidiary by means of transfer pricing.

d The provisions of section 478 of TA 1970 may be invoked to enable the UK Revenue to tax *individuals* ordinarily resident in the UK who are shareholders in the UK company on the profits accumulated in the foreign subsidiary. It should be noted however that section 478 cannot be used to attribute the income of the subsidiary to a UK *company* and thus the section can never be applied to a UK parent with foreign resident shareholders. Furthermore, the section would not generally apply to UK individuals who are shareholders in a UK public quoted company because the exemption in section 478(3) would normally apply. Thus, subject to the provisions listed above, it can be said that generally UK tax is not levied on profits accumulated in foreign subsidiaries of UK public quoted companies. Indeed it is submitted that UK tax could not be levied on the profits even if the subsidiary lent them to the parent provided that the loan was not a sham.

B Unilateral relief

Section 498 allows unilateral relief for foreign taxes by way of credit against UK tax on the same income.[37] Section 498(4) allows relief for underlying corporation tax suffered in respect of dividends from foreign countries provided that the UK company owns at least ten per cent of the voting power. This relief for underlying tax suffered on second-tier and subsequent-tier companies is without limit provided that the UK parent

---

9.36 Which restricts migration of companies from the UK.
9.37 See particularly section 498(3).

has indirect voting power of at least ten per cent in the company which has suffered the underlying corporation tax in respect of which relief is claimed.

C   In respect of which taxes is double taxation relief available?

1   To which types of taxes does it apply?

Generally it applies to taxes on income and profits and sometimes taxes on capital gains, but in the case of UK relief net foreign payroll taxes, net worth taxes rates levied on land values and the like.

In the case of relief granted by treaty, it will depend upon the terms of the treaty which foreign taxes qualify for relief.

In the case of the UK/Belgian treaty the Belgian taxes which qualify for relief are listed in article II, paragraph 1 (b) which can be signified by the general descriptions of income tax and corporation tax.

Unilateral relief under TA 1970 section 498 extends to foreign taxes 'which are charged on income and correspond to income tax or corporation tax in the United Kingdom'.[38]

2   Does it apply to taxes levied by subordinate taxing authorities in the foreign country

Clearly, double taxation relief is available in respect of taxes levied by the supreme legislative body of the country concerned, but the question arises whether relief also extends to taxes levied by provinces forming part of a federal state such as the Swiss cantons or the German länder, and further whether it applies to taxes levied by local municipalities such as town councils.

As with sovereign federal taxes, UK relief is confined to taxes on income or profits, and the question at issue here is whether relief extends to local taxes on income or profits.

In the case of relief under treaties the answer will depend upon the terms of the treaty; for example, relief for Swiss tax extends to 'federal cantonal and communal taxes on income'[39] and 'any other taxes of a

---

9.38 See section 498 (6).
9.39 See UK/Swiss Treaty article I, paragraph (1) (b) – Double Taxation Relief (Taxes on Income) (Switzerland) Order 1955 (SI 1955 No. 422) as amended by the Double Taxation Relief (Taxes on Income) (Switzerland) Order 1967 (SI 1967 No. 26).

substantially similar character imposed subsequently to the date of signature of the Convention'.[40]

Unilateral relief under TA 1970, section 498 applies not only to federal taxes on income, but also to taxes *on income* 'payable under the law of a province, state or other part of a country or levied by or on behalf of a municipality or other local body.[41] [42]

D Three examples of the UK arrangements

Example 1. A UK resident company with a branch in the Netherlands. Company A, resident in the UK carries on a trade in the Netherlands through a branch. The tax treatment of a profit of 100 accruing to the Netherlands branch would be as follows. The branch would constitute a permanent establishment in the Netherlands for the purposes of the tax treaty between the UK and the Netherlands[43] and therefore the treaty permits the Netherlands tax authorities to tax the profits of that permanent establishment.[44] The profit of 100 will therefore be subjected to Dutch corporation tax at 48% under the provisions of the Netherlands tax code. Payments by a branch to the company are not treated as dividends under the Netherlands system and so no Dutch withholding tax will be payable on the branch profit remitted to the parent. Company A is resident in the UK and will therefore be liable under UK domestic tax law to UK corporation tax on the profits accruing to it.[45] Thus in the absence of double tax relief that branch profit of 100 would be subjected to UK corporation tax at 52%. Under article 26 (1) (a) of the treaty the Netherlands tax of 48 is allowed as a credit against company A's

---

9.40 UK/Swiss treaty article I, paragraph (2).
9.41 See section 498 (6).
9.42 For the benefit of foreign readers we would add that under the UK system all taxes on income are 'federal' taxes. The 'provinces' of Scotland and Wales and Northern Ireland do not levy any taxes. Local government authorities finance their operations partly out of grants from the UK central government (made out of the revenue raised by 'federal taxes') and partly out of a local tax levied by the local authorities on the value of land in their area called 'rates' which are thus not a tax on income. The Channel Islands and the Isle of Man are separate tax jurisdictions which are not part of the UK for tax purposes.
9.43 SI 1968 No. 577, article 52(a).
9.44 See ibid. article 8.
9.45 TA 1970, section 238(1) and (4) and section 250. Since company A is resident in the UK and controls the trade carried on by means of the branch, the profit will be computed in accordance with the rules applicable to schedule D case I.

liability to UK corporation tax of 52, leaving a net liability to UK corporation tax of 4.

Example 2. A UK resident company with a branch in France. Company A, resident in the UK carries on a trade in France through a branch. The tax treatment of a profit of 100 accruing to the French branch would be as follows. Under the French tax code that profit of 100 would be liable to French corporation tax at 50%,[46] leaving 50 after French corporation tax has been paid. In addition the French system subjects the remaining 50 to withholding tax as if it were a dividend. The normal rate of withholding tax would be 25%, but the effect of article 10 of the treaty is to reduce that withholding tax to 10%.[47] Thus the total French tax will be 50 (corporation tax) + 5 (withholding tax) = 55. Again that profit of 100 would, in the absence of double tax relief, be liable to UK corporation tax of 52. Article 24(a)(i) provides that the French tax is allowed a credit against UK corporation tax liability. The UK corporation tax liability will therefore be nil and there will be an unused credit of 3.

Example 3. A UK resident company with a subsidiary company in France. Company A resident in the UK owns all the shares in company B, resident in France. Company B carries on a trade in France. Company A has no permanent establishment in France within the meaning of the double tax treaty and has no source of income other than dividends which it receives from company B. Company B has a trading profit of 100 and after paying French tax distributes the balance of that profit to company A. Company B will be liable to French corporation tax of 50 on that dividend and the remaining 50 constitutes the gross dividend which it distributes to company A. That dividend would, apart from double tax relief, be subjected to French withholding tax of 25%, but the treaty reduces that to 5%.[48] The total French tax is thus 50

9.46 Again as the branch would constitute a permanent establishment in France this charge to tax would be permitted by the tax treaty between the UK and France (SI 1969), see articles 4(2)(b) and 6.

9.47 Article 10 provides that the withholding tax in these circumstances shall not exceed 15% of 2/3rds of the profits of the permanent establishment, i.e. in this case

$$\frac{2 \times 50 \times 15}{3 \times 100}$$

9.48 The rate is 5% because company A owns at least 10% of the voting control – article 9 (2)(a). If company A owned less than 10% the withholding tax would be 15% – article 9(2)(b).

(corporation tax) + 2.50 (withholding tax of 5% on the dividend of 50) = 52.50. Apart from any relief for foreign tax by way of credit company A would be liable to corporation tax at 52% on that dividend of 50. The treaty allows company A a credit not only for the French withholding tax of 2.50, but also for the underlying French corporation tax charged on company B.[49]

The relief for the underlying tax is calculated as follows: company B's profit of 100 (which is the gross profit out of which the dividend was paid) is deemed to be company A's and UK corporation tax is calculated on that profit, i.e. 52. All the French tax, both the withholding tax of 2.50 and the underlying corporation tax of 50 is allowed as a credit against the notional liability of 52.[50]

9.49 See article 24(a)(ii). Company A satisfies the requirement of holding at least 10% of the voting stock.
9.50 Article 24(a)(ii) combined with TA 1970, section 506.

10. International double taxation relief under the US and Dutch systems.

In this chapter it is proposed to consider some aspects of the US and Dutch double taxation arrangements. Those two systems have been selected because they provide a contrast to the UK arrangements and because each of them is host to a large number of holding companies forming part of multinational groups. In the case of Holland the holding company is often the European parent of a group having an ultimate parent located elsewhere.

The US has a credit system of double taxation relief, but it has a method of calculating the maximum credit for foreign tax which is different from the UK method. The UK system requires each source of foreign income to be dealt with separately, even in cases where there are two or more sources of foreign income situated in the same foreign country. Under the UK arrangements a credit will be allowed for tax levied in the country of origin on income from a source located there, but that credit can only be set against the UK tax chargeable on the income from *that* source. Thus if a UK company receives a dividend from a source state X which has suffered state X tax at 60%[1] and also receives royalties derived from a state X source which have suffered tax at 10%, there will be no UK corporation tax on the dividend because the state X tax exceeds the UK rate of 52%, but the royalties will be liable to UK corporation tax at an effective rate of 42%[2] and it will not be possible to set the surplus double tax credit in respect of the dividend against UK corporation tax liability on the royalties. *A fortiori* it will be impossible to set a surplus double tax credit in respect of income from one foreign source against UK tax liability on another foreign source where the two sources concerned are situated in different foreign

---

10.1 It is postulated that this figure of 60% comprises dividend withholding tax and underlying corporation tax which qualifies for relief.

10.2 i.e. UK corporation tax at 52% minus a credit for the 10% state X tax.

countries. Those limitations do not exist under the US system which calculates the maximum credit either on a per country basis or on an overall basis, but unlike the UK not upon a per source basis.

Holland 'which has an exemption system of double taxation relief' is regarded in some quarters as an attractive location for the European parent company of a multinational group. The features of the Dutch system which are said to justify this conclusion are: first the participation exemption under which (subject to certain criteria being satisfied) intercorporate dividends (whether received from Dutch or foreign subsidiaries) are exempt from corporation tax in the hands of the Dutch parent; secondly, the favourable network of treaties under which income flows into and out of Holland are in some instances subject to lower rates of withholding tax than those which are exigible under treaties between other countries and, thirdly, the Dutch holding company can dispose of any of its shareholdings to which the participation exemption applies without any liability to tax in respect of capital gains.

A   Aspects of the US system.

The US has a classical system of corporation tax with a basic corporate tax rate of 22% plus a corporate surtax of 26% on taxable income over $25,000. Thus except in the case of companies with small profits, the US corporate tax rate can be taken to be approximately 48%. Dividends are subject to personal income tax in the hands of individual shareholders; no tax is deducted at source from dividends paid to US residents, but dividends paid to foreign residents are subject to deduction of withholding tax at 30% or a reduced rate if a double tax treaty so provides.

1   Calculation of allowable credit

A broad outline of the system of calculating the maximum permissible credit has been given in the introduction to this chapter.

a The per country basis. In the case of the per country basis a maximum credit for foreign tax has to be calculated for each country and that maximum will be an amount equal to US tax on all the taxpayer's income from all sources in the country concerned grossed-up by reference to the foreign tax which has been levied in that country. The following examples illustrate the operation of the per country basis.

Example 1. A US corporation receives income from two sources located in state X, dividends from a subsidiary company resident there and royalties received from a person resident in state X under an agreement governed by the law of that state. The net dividend received by the US corporation was 40 which had suffered state X tax[3] at 60% and the net royalty was 90 which had been subjected to state X withholding tax at 10%. The dividend grossed-up by reference to the state X tax is 100 and the royalty thus grossed-up is 100. US tax at 48% on the gross of 200 derived from state X is 96 and therefore the maximum amount of state X tax which will be allowed as a credit against US tax liability on the state X income is 96. The total state X tax is 70 and therefore the limit is not exceeded and the US tax computation is as follows:

Income from state X (grossed-up)	=	200
US tax is 48% on 200	=	96
Minus credit for state X tax (60 + 10)	=	70
net US liability	=	26

Example 2. Assume the same facts as example 1 except that the dividend suffered state X tax at 70% and the royalty a state X withholding tax at 30%. The maximum credit for state X on the per country basis is 96 and the total state X tax is 100. The US tax computation is as follows:

Income from state X (grossed-up)	=	200
US tax is 48% on 200	=	96
Minus credit for state X tax (70 + 30)		
= 100 limited to		96
net US liability		Nil

The unused credit of 4 cannot be set against US tax charged on sources located in other countries, but it can be carried backwards for two years and forward for five years and set against US liability on income from state X sources in those years subject always to the maxima applicable in those years.[4]

b The overall basis. In the case of the overall basis the maximum credit for foreign tax is calculated on world-wide foreign source income and

---

10.3 Comprising dividend withholding tax and underlying corporate tax. The US gives relief for underlying tax charged on subsidiaries.

10.4 Surplus credit cannot be carried over from a year in which the taxpayer has elected for the per country basis into a year in which he has elected for the overall basis or *vice versa*.

that maximum will be an amount equal to US tax on all the taxpayer's foreign source income from all countries grossed-up in each case by the foreign tax which has been levied on it.[5] The following example illustrates the overall basis.

Example 3. A US corporation receives income from sources in states X and Y. Its foreign source income comprises

(i) A net dividend from a subsidiary company resident in state X of 40 which has suffered state X tax (including underlying tax) at 70%,

(ii) A net royalty paid by a person resident in state X under an agreement governed by state X law of 70 which has suffered state X tax at 30%, and

(iii) Net income from a branch located in state Y of 80 which has suffered state Y tax at 20%.

The US corporation's total foreign source income grossed-up by reference to the relevant foreign taxes is:

State X	200
State Y	100
	300

The maximum credit calculated on the overall basis is 48% of 300 = 144
The US tax computation is as follows:

Foreign source income grossed-up	=	300
US tax at 48% on 300	=	144
Minus credit for foreign tax of 100[6]		
(state X) + 20 (state Y)	=	120
Net US tax liability	=	24

c Election between the per country basis and the overall basis. The taxpayer must elect for the per country basis or the overall basis and once an election has been made, the taxpayer cannot generally elect for a different basis in subsequent years without the consent of the Internal Revenue Service.[7]

10.5 Surplus credit can be carried back two years and forward five years subject to the limitation set out in footnote 4 above.
10.6 i.e. 70 withholding and underlying tax in respect of the dividend and 30 withholding tax on the royalty.
10.7 The fiscal authority in the US.

2   Relief for underlying tax

The US double taxation system gives relief by way of credit in respect of underlying tax suffered by companies in which it owns shares provided that the US taxpayer owns 10% or more of the voting stock. Relief is also available for underlying tax suffered by second-tier companies and third-tier companies, but not beyond. In the case of second and third-tier companies, each company in the line must hold ten per cent or more of the voting stock in the company below it, and the top company[8] must have through the intermediary companies at least 5% interest in the bottom company.[9]

3   Taxation of income of foreign subsidiaries not repatriated to the US

Until 1962 the US provisions dealing with this practice were confined to provisions similar to those which exist in the UK, but in 1962 provisions were introduced into the Internal Revenue Code[10] whereby certain income of foreign companies controlled[11] by US shareholders, whether individuals, or private or public companies is attributed to the US shareholder(s) and taxed in their hands whether the income is repatriated or not. The income concerned is known as subpart F income and comprises in particular income derived by the foreign subsidiary from cross-invoicing or from the supply of services.[12]

Thus, unlike the UK the US system sometimes taxes unrepatriated profits accumulated in foreign subsidiaries of US public companies.

4   The new UK/US Double Tax Treaty

The principal change which this treaty makes in the double taxation relief on income flows between these two countries is the provision relating to dividends.[13]

As regards dividends flowing from the UK to the US, the UK has had to agree to repay half the tax credit, subject to a withholding tax of 5%,

---

10.8 i.e. the US corporation which is claiming the relief.
10.9 i.e. the company which has paid the foreign corporation tax in respect of which the relief for underlying tax is being claimed.
10.10 IRC section 951.
10.11 In the relevant sense; usually 50% of the voting stock constitutes control, see IRC section 957.
10.12 For a detailed description of the subpart F provisions and the US treatment of foreign source income, see the article by David R. Tillinghast in 29 NYU Inst on Fed Tax, page 1.
10.13 Draft SI 1976, article 10.

where the US shareholder is a company owning 10% or more of the voting power in the UK company.[14]

As regards dividends flowing from the US to the UK, they will be subject to a US withholding tax at 15%,[15] except where the UK company controls 10% or more of the voting stock in the US company in which case the withholding tax is limited to 5%.[16]

B Aspects of the Dutch system

Holland has a classical system of corporation tax with a corporate tax rate of 48%. Holland has an exemption system of double taxation of the type known as exemption with progression. The broad effect of this is that foreign source income which has been taxed in the origin country is exempt from Dutch tax, but that foreign source income can be taken into account in determining the progressive rate applicable to the taxpayer's Dutch income. Thus if a Dutch individual has income, 30% of which is foreign source income which has been taxed in the origin country and 70% of which is income from Dutch sources, Dutch tax is calculated on his world-wide income, but tax is reduced by the proportion which his Dutch income bears to his world-wide income i.e. in this case the Dutch tax chargeable is 70% of the tax which would (but for the exemption) be payable on his world-wide income.

Since companies are taxed at a flat rate under the Dutch system, the exemption with progression produces the same result as a straightforward exemption system in the case of foreign source income accruing to a Netherlands company.

Holland is often said to be a favourable situs for holding companies and it is now proposed to examine briefly some of the features of the Dutch system which are considered to give rise to these advantages.

1   Treatment of dividend income received by a Netherlands parent company from a foreign subsidiary: '

The treatment of such income will depend on a feature of the Dutch tax system known as the participation exemption. Its operation in purely domestic cases will be explained before considering its effect in cases involving foreign elements.

10.14 For details see chapter 9.
10.15 Which was the case under the old treaty.
10.16 This provision is new. See article 10, paragraph 2 (b) of the new treaty.

a Operation of the participation exemption in domestic cases. Where a Netherlands company holds shares in another company which constitute at least 5% of the paid-up capital of that other company, the participation exemption will apply. The effect of the exemption is that the recipient company will not be liable to corporation tax on the dividends it has received from the other company. Where both companies are resident in Holland the paying company will have suffered Dutch corporation tax on the profits from which it has paid the dividend.

Thus in a purely domestic Dutch case the participation exemption serves the same purpose as the franked investment income and group provisions in a domestic UK case. The recipient company's liability to Dutch corporation tax on the dividend is franked by the underlying corporation tax paid by the company paying the dividend.

b Effect of the participation exemption in cases of foreign source dividends. The Dutch participation exemption can also apply to cases where the company paying the dividend is not resident in Holland, provided that two additional criteria are satisfied, namely
(i) that the company paying the dividend must have some liability to pay corporation tax on the underlying profits and
(ii) the company receiving the dividend must hold its shares in the paying company as a business holding rather than a portfolio investment. Thus if a Dutch company holds in the ordinary course of its business shares in a subsidiary resident abroad, dividends received by the Dutch company from that foreign subsidiary which are paid out of the subsidiary's taxed profits will be exempt from Dutch corporation tax.

This can be regarded simply as a feature of the domestic Dutch tax code and therefore not a form of double taxation relief at all. On the other hand, the authors take the view that, in the case of dividends received from outside Holland, the participation is a form of unilateral relief by way of exemption on a destination basis. In support of this the authors would point out: one, that the liability to Dutch corporation tax is being franked not by underlying Dutch corporation tax, but by underlying foreign corporation tax; two, the rate of underlying foreign corporation tax may be lower than the Dutch rate and yet the participation exemption is not affected; and three, in the case of foreign dividends additional criteria have to be satisfied before the participation exemption can apply.

Whichever explanation be adopted, it was felt appropriate to deal with the participation exemption at this point, in order to provide a comparison between the Dutch treatment of foreign source dividend income and the UK treatment.

c *The difference between a holding of shares in the ordinary course of business and a portfolio investment for the purposes of the participation exemption.* In a recent decision of the Netherlands Supreme Court (dated 4 November 1973) this question was considered. The facts were that individuals resident in Holland held the shares in a Netherlands company which had wholly owned subsidiaries in the Netherlands and abroad. The participation exemption applied to the dividends derived from the Netherlands subsidiaries, but the Supreme Court held that the participation exemption did not apply to the dividends from the foreign subsidiaries on the ground that the Netherlands company was purely a holding company and therefore held the shares in those foreign subsidiaries as a portfolio investment and not in the ordinary course of its business.

This decision caused concern because, at first sight, it would also apply to a multinational group having a Dutch holding company which merely held shares in foreign subsidiaries and did not itself carry on any trade. It was felt in some quarters that the Dutch economy might be significantly adversely affected if this caused multinational groups to site their European holding companies elsewhere. After some speculation about the effects of this decision, questions raised in the Dutch Parliament elucidated assurances that this decision will not apply to Dutch holding companies forming part of multinational groups. It seems that a shareholding will be within the participation exemption if the shares are held in the ordinary course of business of the Dutch holding company or of its parent.

2 Withholding taxes on income flowing through the Netherlands

Under the Dutch system no withholding taxes are exacted on interest, royalties and service fees. Dividends are subjected to a withholding tax of 25%, but this will be reduced under double tax treaties.

The double tax treaties between Holland and other countries often provide for rates of withholding tax which are lower than the rates which are prescribed in tax treaties between other countries. It is, therefore, sometimes possible to save withholding tax by routing income through the Netherlands.

3 Disposals of foreign subsidiaries

Where a Dutch company disposes of the shares in a subsidiary, whether Dutch or foreign, then, if it is a case where the participation exemption applies, there is no tax on any capital gain accruing on the disposal of those shares. This, of course, is not always an advantage, if the shares are worth less than their acquisition cost, tax relief for a capital loss will not be available on a disposal of those shares, except where the subsidiary is being liquidated. The exemption from taxation on capital gains in respect of a disposal of the shares in the subsidiary is regarded as an advantage in case fiscal, economic or political changes make it desirable to dispose of the subsidiary.

11. A discussion of the overspill problem

This chapter will be devoted to a consideration of what is called the overspill problem.

A Introduction

In the authors' experience the expression 'overspill' is used in at least two different senses. One possible meaning of overspill is the problem of a taxpayer company having a credit for foreign tax which is larger than its corporation tax liability in the destination country so that is has unused and unusable tax credit. Overspill in this sense is a feature which can only occur where the destination country has a credit system of double tax relief. A second and wider meaning of overspill is the phenomenon of profits derived from multinational enterprises being subjected to a more severe total tax burden[1] than that suffered in the case of profits derived from domestic enterprises of either country. Overspill in this sense can arise whether the destination country has a credit or an exemption system of double tax relief. Whether there is such an overspill will depend upon the rates of corporation tax and the rates of tax on dividends imposed by each of the countries concerned. Examples 1 and 2 below illustrate this.

In the remainder of this chapter the word 'overspill' will be used in the second and wider sense. Since such an overspill can arise under both the credit and the exemption systems of double tax relief the first question which arises is, why is it that the overspill problem is such a conspicuous source of complaint in the UK which has a credit system

---

11.1 The phrase 'total tax burden' is used to mean corporation tax and personal income tax on distributions.

but not in European countries which have exemption systems. The authors feel that probably the main reason why the overspill problem has excited so much debate in the UK is that under the pre-1965 UK company tax system overspill was obviated by the net UK rate provisions.[2] When the UK adopted a classical system of corporation tax in 1965 and abandoned the net UK rate an overspill was suffered by UK companies for the first time and the overspill has been further exacerbated under the UK imputation system.

The principal cause of overspill in the wide sense is that, although the recipient company will have a credit or exemption which obviates any destination country corporation tax on the foreign income, no credit or exemption is carried through to the shareholders who will therefore pay full personal income tax on dividends derived from that foreign income.[3] Those who subscribe to the view that the taxation of the company should be considered separately from taxation of the shareholders because they are separate legal persons will not find anything objectionable in this failure to carry the double tax relief through to the shareholders in the destination country. As the authors have already indicated,[4] they subscribe to the hypothesis that one should have regard to the total tax burden of corporate tax and personal income tax. The authors therefore regard the overspill as undesirable in principle and will suggest ways in which it might be mitigated.

B Examples illustrating the overspill problem

It is assumed, unless otherwise indicated, that in each example used in this section the shareholders are liable to personal income tax at only the basic rate.

1 *Where the destination country has a credit system of double tax relief*

Example 1. Company A, resident in state X, owns all the shares in company B, resident in state Y. Each state has a classical system of corporation tax with a rate of 40%. The double tax treaty between two states provides for a withholding tax of 10% on dividends passing between those states. State X grants relief for underlying tax in the same manner as the UK.[5] Each state has a basic rate of personal income tax of 30%.

11.2 The broad effect of these will be explained below.
11.3 See chapter 7.
11.4 See chapter 2.
11.5 See chapter 9.

tate X

Company A receives 54 from company B. That must be grossed-up for the purpose of calculating the DTR.
Corporation tax liability of company A=

100 at 40%	= 40
less DTR	46
	NIL

Unused DTR 6.
Company A then distributes that 54 to its shareholders and their personal income tax liability will be 54 at 30% = 16.2.
The shareholders will therefore receive 37.8.

State Y

Company B has a profit of 100 on which it pays corporation tax of 40. It resolves to distribute the remaining 60 to its parent.
The withholding tax on that dividend will be 6.
Total state Y tax = 46
Net amount distributed to company A = 54.

The total tax burden on that income flow is therefore 62.2%, as compare with a total burden of 58%[6] in the case of purely domestic investment in either state X or state Y. If the country of origin has a higher rate of corporation tax than the destination country then the prejudice to the multinational company caused by the overspill is even greater, unless the rate of personal income tax in state X is sufficiently lower than the rate of personal income tax in state Y so as to counterbalance the disadvantage of the unusable tax credit.

If, for instance, state Y had an imputation system of corporation tax in example 1, but state X had a classical system, the overspill problem could be even more severe. Countries operating an imputation system of corporation tax tend to have higher rates of corporation tax than countries operating classical systems. State Y would therefore be likely to have a corporation tax rate of about 50%. In the case of domestic shareholders this is mitigated by the tax credit which is inherent in the imputation system. The system of double tax relief under discussion does not allow the state Y tax credit to be carried over to the shareholders in company A. Thus in these circumstances the unused double tax relief is increased from 6 to 15, the state Y tax credit is not carried over to the individual shareholders in state X, nor can they set

11.6 i.e. corporation tax at 40% on 100 + personal income of 30% on the 60 available for distribution 40 + 18 = 58.

the unused double tax credit against their liability to personal income tax. The figures as as follows:

State X		*State Y*	
45 grossed-up by reference to underlying tax	= 100	Profit	100
Corporation tax	= 40	Corporation tax of	50
Less DTR	55	Withholding tax	5
Unused DTR	15	Net distribution	45
Personal income tax of 30% of 45 + 13.5			

Total tax burden is 55 (state Y) + 13.50 (state X) =68.5%.

What then are the possible solutions to this overspill problem? It could be suggested that company A be allowed to set the unused double tax credit against corporation tax liability in earlier or later accounting periods. This would not, however, cure the problem unless in those accounting periods company A had a large enough liability to corporation tax in respect of domestic income to use up that credit. Thus if company A's income remained totally foreign it would have a permanent unrelieved overspill.

Another possible suggestion is to allow the shareholders in company A to set the unused double tax credit against their liability to personal income tax. The objection to this is that it reduces the amount of tax collected by state X and could involve the state X revenue refunding to an exempt shareholder tax which it never collected. Suppose that in example 1 the unused tax credit of 6 could be set against the personal income tax liability of the individual shareholders in company A. In order to prevent the shareholders obtaining a greater relief than they should have it would be necessary for state X to treat that credit of 6 as part of the shareholders taxable income.[7] Their personal income tax liability on that dividend would therefore be 30% of (54 (dividend) + 6 (tax credit))= 18 − 6 (tax credit)= 12. If the shareholders in company A were exempt taxpayers, they would seek to have the tax they had suffered repaid. Logically they ought to be repaid the full basic rate tax of 18 since this represents the tax they have actually paid, 12 plus the tax credit of 6 to which they are entitled. If the state X tax code does require payment of the full 18, the state X Revenue will be refunding 18 having exacted only 12. The other solution to this difficulty is for state X to limit the amount which can be recovered by the shareholders, so that the

---

11.7 If this were not done the total tax burden would be: state Y tax of 40 (corporation tax) + 6 (withholding tax)= 46 + state X personal income tax of 16.2 (i.e. 30% of 54) − 6= 10.2, making a total of 56.2%.

state X revenue does not have to repay more than it has collected. This latter system operated in the UK before 1965, in the form of limiting the amount which an exempt shareholder could recover to the net UK rate of tax suffered by the UK company paying the dividend. The former system is proposed in the EEC draft Directive on Harmonisation of Corporate Taxes together with provisions for financial compensation between member states.

2 Where the destination country has an exemption system of double tax relief

Example 2. Company A, resident in state X, owns all the shares in company B, resident in state Y. Each state has a classical system of corporation tax with a rate of 40%. The double tax treaty between the two states provides for a withholding tax of 10% on dividends passing between those states. State X has an exemption system of double tax relief. Each state has a basic rate of personal income tax of 30%.

State X	*State Y*
Company A receives 54 from company B. Company A is exempt from corporation tax on that 54. Company A then distributes that 54 to its shareholders whose personal income tax will be 30% of 54 = 16.2	Company B has a profit of 100 on which it pays corporation tax of 40. It resolves to distribute the remaining 60 to its parent. withholding tax = 6. Total state Y tax = 46 Net dividend = 54.

Thus the total burden of tax on that income flow is 62.2% compared with 58% in the case of a purely domestic case.[8] Those who take the view that the taxation of the company should be divorced from the taxation of the shareholders may find these results unexceptional, but according to the authors' hypotheses[9] the overspill in this case is objectionable. The authors submit that a solution to this overspill which is consistent with relief by way of exemption is to exempt the dividend paid by company B to company A from state Y withholding tax. Thus state Y tax would be corporation tax of 40 and the net dividend of 60 would be exempt from corporation tax in state X, but liable to state X personal income tax of 18 when distributed to the shareholders in company A, making a total tax burden of 58%.

Whatever may be the continental view, the overspill problem has given rise to a considerable furore in the UK and in the following section the UK position will be examined more closely.

11.8 i.e. The same results as in example 1 above.
11.9 Namely that regard should be had to the total burden of corporate tax on profits and personal income tax on distributions and that multinational enterprises should not bear a greater burden of tax than domestic enterprises.

C   The overspill problem in the UK

As we indicated in the introduction overspill problems generally did not arise in the UK under the pre-1965 system of corporate tax. It is now proposed to demonstrate how this occurred and then to trace the development of the overspill problem after 1965. Again it is assumed unless otherwise indicated that in each example used in this section the shareholders are liable to personal income tax at only the basic rate.[10]

1   The pre-1965 position

Under the pre-1965 UK corporate tax system the profits of companies were subjected to income tax and profits tax. When a company paid a dividend it was entitled to deduct income tax[11] from the dividend and retain the tax deducted. The shareholders thus received the dividend under deduction of tax and a shareholder who was not liable to that tax[12] could make a repayment claim.[13] Where a UK company paid a dividend out of foreign source income upon which it had not suffered income tax and profits tax in full because of a credit for foreign tax, the company was nevertheless entitled to deduct and retain income tax[14] on that dividend.

Example 1. In 1965–6 company A, resident in the UK, received a net dividend of 54 from a foreign subsidiary. The foreign tax on that income flow was withholding tax of 6 and underlying corporation tax of 40. The dividend grossed-up by reference to the foreign tax[15] amounted to 100. In that year the standard rate of income tax was 41.25% and the rate of profits tax was 15%.

Company A's tax liability		
Dividend (grossed-up)	=	100
Income tax liability	=	41.25
Profits tax liability	=	15.00
Total tax liability	=	56.25
Minus DTR of		46
		10.25

11.10 Before 1973 this was called the 'standard rate' in the UK terminology.
11.11 At the standard rate.
11.12 e.g. because of an exemption or unused personal reliefs.
11.13 For a domestic example of the pre-1965 system see chapter 2.
11.14 At the standard rate.
11.15 i.e. corporation tax at 40% plus withholding tax at 10%.

Net amount available for distribution	=	43.75
Gross dividend	=	74.47
Tax at the standard rate of 41.25% on 74.47	=	30.72
(This is deducted and retained by company A)		
Net dividend	=	43.75

Thus the total burden of tax on this income flow was 40 (foreign corporation tax) + 6 (foreign withholding tax) + 10.25 (UK income and profits tax) = 56.25. In a purely domestic case the total burden would also be 56.25 (comprising 41.25 UK income tax + UK profits tax). There would only be an overspill problem if the total foreign tax exceeded 56.25% which would not be a very common occurrence.

What was the position if the shareholders in company A were exempt from tax? If they were able to recover the full 30.72 which was deducted by company A at source when paying the dividend, the UK would be refunding 30.72 having collected only 10.25. For obvious reasons this was not permitted and instead the repayment claim was limited by reference to what was known as the net UK rate.[16] The calculation of the net UK rate was immensely complicated,[17] but it is sufficient for present purposes to state that the effect of net UK rate rules was to prevent the exempt shareholders in company A from recovering more than the UK tax actually paid by company A. Thus it was not to the advantage of an exempt person (e.g. a charity or pension fund) to invest in shares of a company having a net UK rate much below the standard rate.

If a company had a credit for foreign tax which was the same as or more than 56.25% then no UK income tax or profits tax would be payable by the UK company on that foreign source income and if that company had no domestic income the net UK rate would be nil.

Example 2. Take the same facts as in example 1 except that the total foreign tax is 57.5.[18]

Company A's liability		
Dividend (grossed-up)	=	100
UK income tax + profits tax	=	56.25
Minus DTR of		57.5
		Nil

11.16 See Income Tax Act 1952, section 350.
11.17 See Double Taxation Relief (Taxes on Income) (General) Regulations 1946 (SI 1946 No. 466) as amended by Double Taxation Relief (Taxes on Income) (General) (No. 2) Regulations 1950 and the example in *British Tax Encyclopedia* para 15–051.
11.18 Comprising corporation tax at 50% plus withholding tax at 15%.

Net amounts available for distribution	=	42.50
Gross dividend	=	72.34
Tax at the standard rate of 41.25% on 72.34	=	29.84
(which is deducted and retained by company A)		
Net dividend	=	42.50

The net UK rate is nil. The position is that if the shareholders in company A are liable only to standard rate they do not have to pay any further tax, whereas if they are exempt they cannot reclaim any of the tax deducted at source.

2 The position under the classical system which operated in the UK between 1965 and 1972

Under this system the rate of corporation tax varied between 37.5% and 45%. To take 1968–69 as an example: the standard rate of income tax was 41.25% and the rate of corporation tax was 45%. Thus corporation tax was 45, and, assuming maximum distributions income tax at 41.25% on the remaining 55 = 22.69, making a total tax burden of 67.69%. The next example illustrates the overspill which would arise in the case of a company with foreign source income.

Example 3. In 1968–69 company A, resident in the UK, received dividend income of 49.5 net of foreign tax from a foreign subsidiary in state X. Postulating that state X had the same tax rates as the UK and that the Double Tax Treaty provided for a state X withholding tax of 10%, the position would be as follows:

State X tax   Corporation tax of 45 + withholding tax at 10% on the balance of 55 = 5.5 giving 50.5.

UK tax   Company A would have to gross-up the dividend by reference to

all the foreign tax	=	100
Corporation tax at 45%	=	45
Minus DTR of		50.5
		————
		Nil
Net amount available for distribution	=	49.5
Standard rate tax at 41.25% on 49.5	=	20.42
Net Dividend	=	29.08

Total tax burden = 50.5 (foreign tax) + 20.42 (UK tax) = 70.92%.

This compares with a total burden of 67.59% in a purely domestic UK or state X case. Thus the overspill problem began to be felt under the post 1965 classical system because the corporation tax rate was not high enough to absorb the credit for foreign tax and there was no carry through of the credit to the shareholders.

3 Position under the post-1973 imputation system

The introduction of the imputation system in 1973 exacerbated the overspill problem for certain UK multinational companies. Two aspects of that imputation system tend to make the overspill problem worse. First, under that system the total burden of tax on distributed profits in domestic cases is lessened by reason of the imputation which thus improves the position of purely domestic enterprises. Secondly, under that system the company is required to set off ACT against its potential liability to corporation tax on its foreign source income before any double tax relief is set off, thus increasing the amount of unusable double tax relief. There is, however, a feature which mitigates the overspill in the case of some companies, namely the rule that the company can elect to set that ACT as far as possible against domestic income to the exclusion of foreign source income. In so far as the ACT has to be set against foreign source income, it must be set off before double tax relief is set off. Thus UK companies with sufficient domestic income to cover their dividends, do not suffer a prejudice under this system, whereas UK companies paying dividends out of foreign source income can suffer a severe overspill problem. This is illustrated in the following example.

Example 4. Company A, resident in the UK, owns all the shares in company B, resident and trading in state X. The shareholders in company A are all resident in the UK. Company A makes up its accounts each year on 31 March. State X has an imputation system of corporation tax with a corporation tax rate of 50% and an imputation of 50% of the net dividend. The Double Tax Treaty between the UK and state X provides for a 10% withholding tax on dividends passing between those countries.

UK	*State X*
In June 1975 company A received 45 from company B and had no other income in the period from 1 April 1975 to 31 March 1976. For DTR purposes that 45 is grossed-up to 100.	Company B has a profit of 100 on which it pays corporation tax of 50. Company B resolves to distribute the remainder to company A. The state X withholding tax will be 5.
UK corporation tax on that 100 would be 52, but various amounts can be set against that potential liability which reduce it to nil (see below).	
If in December 1975 company A paid the maximum dividend to its	

shareholders out of that 45, the dividend received by the shareholders would have been 29.25 on which company A would be liable to pay ACT of 35/65ths of 29.25 = 15.75.

Company A's corporation tax liability is:

	52	
Minus	15.75	ACT
	36.25	
Minus	55	DTR
	Nil	
Unused DTR	18.75	

Total tax burden on that income flow, on the assumption that the shareholders in company A were liable to income tax at only the basic rate would be 70.75 (comprising state X tax of 55, UK ACT of 15.75). In a purely domestic UK case the total burden of tax would be 52% if the shareholders were liable to income tax at only the basic rate. In a purely domestic state X case postulating a basic rate of personal income tax of 35% and shareholders who were liable to tax at only that rate the total tax burden would be as follows:

Corporation tax	= 50
Net amount available for distribution	= 50
Imputation	= 25
Total gross dividend	= 75
	(50 + imputation of 25)
Tax on that at 35%	= 26.25
Tax credit (Imputation)	= 25

The shareholders would thus be liable to pay income tax of 1.25. The total tax burden is therefore corporation tax of 50 plus income tax of 1.25 = 51.25.

Thus on these facts and under the present UK system a profit of 100 made by the foreign subsidiary puts 29.25 into the pockets of shareholders liable to personal income tax at 35%. This compares with 48 in a purely domestic UK case and 48.75 in a purely domestic state X case.

The reason why the UK system has not caused more furore than it has, is because those multinational companies which have sufficient UK income to cover their dividends are not prejudiced by the system. Those UK companies with predominantly foreign income can be severely prejudiced.[19]

11.19 The UK legislation provides some temporary relief against overspill, see p. 124.

D   Conclusions on the overspill problem

The opinion of the authors is that the prejudice caused by the overspill problem is neither justifiable nor need it be inevitable. Any system which results in a multinational company bearing a burden of tax greater than that borne by domestic enterprises of the countries in which it operates interferes with competition and may lead to inefficient allocation of resources, although it may be defensible from the viewpoint of national interest. The UK Revenue is firmly opposed to a return to the net UK rate system.[20] The reasons put forward for this are: first, that the system was complex, secondly that it enables foreign countries to charge high taxes on British interests at the expense of the UK Revenue, and thirdly that it distorts the capital market because under that system exempt shareholders such as pension funds and charities would suffer the disadvantage of having only a limited repayment claim if they invest in companies with a considerable amount of foreign source income. The authors are unconvinced by the arguments based on complexity. The Revenue is quite prepared to countenance complex anti-avoidance provisions[21] and therefore it is submitted that they owe a corresponding duty to tolerate complexity in the interests of equity. As to the second argument, the authors' opinion is that it is questionable whether foreign countries in fact fix their corporation tax rate by reference to the UK system of relief for foreign tax but even if they do, this does not substantiate an argument for a particular system until it is shown that the overall outcome is that most advantageous from the point of view of national interest.

As to the argument that it distorts the capital market, the authors would point out that so does the present UK system. Under that system UK companies deriving their income mainly from operations through foreign subsidiaries will have to earn more profits than their UK domestic competitors in order to pay the same net dividend to their UK shareholders. If they are unable to do this, their dividends will be smaller which will make their shares less attractive and thus distort the capital market. The authors would argue that it is preferable to tolerate a distortion arising out of an equitable system of double taxation rather than out of an inequitable one. An analogy to the net UK rate system exists in the domestic UK tax code. Interest paid by approved building societies is paid net of basic rate tax and the society accounts to the Revenue for an amount of tax which is designed to cover what would

---

11.20 See Minutes of Evidence taken before the Select Committee on Corporation Tax (cmd. 1971 No. 622) pages 1 and 2, 20 and 21.
11.21 TA 1970 sections 460 and 478 to mention but two.

otherwise have been the net yield to the Revenue if that interest had been taxed in the hands of the investors. It is, however, expressly provided that exempt investors cannot make a repayment claim and yet it has never been suggested that this tax treatment produces an unacceptable distortion of the capital market.

When the net UK rate system was abandoned in 1965, some transitional relief was given against overspill and in 1972 the period for which this relief was to last was extended.[22]

The proposals in the EEC Working Paper on Harmonisation of Corporate Taxes will, if adopted, obviate the overspill problem in the case of income flows within the EEC but the problem will remain in the case of income coming to the UK from non-EEC countries. It is essential to the functioning of the new system proposed for the EEC that each state should have an imputation system and that the rates of corporation tax and tax credits are kept within fairly narrow bands. Because of these features, this proposed system is not suitable for use outside the EEC.

The opinion of the authors is that the pre-1965 net UK rate system is preferable to the present system which imposes an unfair burden on those UK companies which have a large amount of foreign source income and therefore the UK ought to revert to that pre-1965 system notwithstanding the complexity of calculating the net UK rate.

11.22 See FA 1965 section 84 as amended by FA 1972, section 99. For a detailed examination of the overspill relief see the article by Dr J.B. Bracewell-Milnes in *European Taxation*, Volume 14, No. 5, May 1974.

12. Governments' reactions to each other in taxation policy towards multinational enterprises

In previous chapters we have outlined various systems of relief from double taxation of multinational enterprises. In this chapter we return to the discussion of chapter 5 where we raised the issue of how governments react to each other's policies in this sphere. While in the past, retaliatory practices along the lines outlined here have not by and large been entered into, increasingly there are signs that governments (particularly in developed economies) are becoming aware of this problem. We would claim that incentives for pursuit of national interest (and hence for retaliatory action) are clearly present in this area. The presence of these incentives has the important implication that many agreements entered into by treaty may well become unacceptable to one party as circumstances break down and renegotiation of fresh treaties may result. The discussion here, in turn, illustrates the motivation for international agreements to be pursued in this area and in the next chapter moves in this direction within the EEC will be taken up. We also comment here on the role of tax havens in the overall tax position of multinational enterprises, tax havens being examples of small jurisdictions who have responded to the tax regimes of developed economies by adopting low or zero tax rates.

A The incentives for governments to respond to each other's actions

An important feature of the tax treatment of multinational enterprises is that tax authorities in various countries as well as multinational enterprises themselves may respond to the actions of tax authorities abroad. By way of example one can quote the recent decision by the

British Government to adopt an imputation system of corporation tax rather than a two-rate system as being motivated by double taxation considerations which affect the tax treatment of subsidiaries of multinational parent companies conducting business in Britain. This decision may clearly be viewed as a response by the UK tax authorities to the tax treatment of multinational enterprises by foreign tax authorities. Equally, the decision[1] by the West German government to consider introducing an element of imputation into their two-rate system could also be viewed as a response to the actions of other tax authorities.

This is a conventional problem in economics involving a small number of participants in a 'game' and an elegant analysis of the problem in the context of the taxation of foreign income has been presented by Hamada.[2] This analysis is pursued here. In a two country model Hamada demonstrates that by reducing the amount of foreign investment from that which would occur with equal tax treatment of domestic and multinational parent companies through a situation with harsher tax treatment applied to multinational enterprises, one country will be able to raise its national income at the expense of the other. Thus, the appropriate tax policy to be adopted towards multinational enterprises by one country depends from a purely nationalist viewpoint on the measures taken by the other country. It seems useful at this point to emphasise this feature by considering Hamada's model and its implications more fully.

We consider a world in which there are only two countries I and II, each country producing only one identical commodity. We will also assume that the amount of labour employed in each country is fixed. Hence a production function relating capital inputs to the quantity of output in each country (I and II) may be written for each country as

$$f_I (K_I - K) \text{ and } f_{II} (K_{II} + K)$$

where K_I, K_{II} are initial amounts of capital 'located' in (owned by) each country and K is the capital exported from country I to country II. Assuming that the marginal productivity of capital diminishes with

---

12.1 The current expectation is that the present two-rate (51% on retentions, 15% (but effectively 23%) on distributions) will be replaced by a 'two-rate, imputation' system with tax rates of 56% on retentions and 36% on distributions (a portion (or with possibly the whole) of the 36% to be imputed as a credit against German personal income tax). This proposed change may possibly be frustrated by moves to harmonise corporate taxes in the EEC, although the completion of such moves by the end of 1976 seems most unlikely at the time of writing.

12.2 K. Hamada 'Strategic Aspects of taxation on foreign investment income'. *Quarterly Journal of Economics* 1966.

further capital employment in each country, then with no taxation imposed by either government marginal productivities of capital in each country would be equalised by market forces. The amount of capital K^* would be sent from I to II where $f_I(K_{II} - K^*) = f_{II}(K_{II} + K^*)$. Diagramatically, this situation is represented in figure 1 where P_I, P_{II} are the marginal product of capital curves in each country. In the absence of taxation, market forces result in a flow of capital between countries up to the point where marginal products are equalised across the countries giving the equilibrium 'flow' of capital K^*. For such an equilibrium the

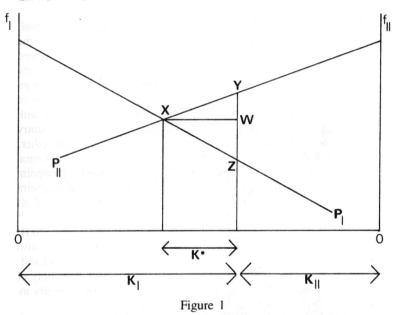

Figure 1

area XYZ represents the gain in world product from the capital flow K^* relative to a situation where no capital flow occurs. The gain is distributed between the countries; XWZ accrues to country I and XWY to country II. From the national viewpoints of countries I and II, however, K^* need not be the best solution and the question of appropriate national tax policy for each country to pursue can be brought into the analysis.

By reducing the flow of capital through tax policy, one country may be able to raise its own income at the expense of the other country. In other words by varying the amount which the country I lends abroad the 'price' on all other capital lent from I to II will change. Thus the marginal cost of borrowing capital for country II (MC) is not just f_I (the

foregone marginal product of capital in country I) but $f_I - Kf_I$. Equally, the marginal revenue (MR) derived from lending capital for country I is $f_{II} + Kf_{II}$. Through tax policy the national governments can charge foreign borrowers the monopoly price for funds, and can pay foreign lenders the monopsony price even though the domestic capital markets are competitive.[3]
These MC and MR curves are drawn in figure 2.

12.3 The situation can be set out more formally as follows:
Let t_{II} be the rate of withholding tax imposed by country II (the borrowing country).
Let s_I be the rate of tax in country I on income from country II net of withholding tax at the rate t_{II}.
Let t_I^* be the rate of tax in country I on domestic income.
Then competitive markets will result in an equalisation of net of tax value marginal products in the two countries, i.e.

(1) $(1 - t_I^*) \ f_I'(K_I - K) = (1 - s_I) \ (1 - t_{II}) \ f_{II}' \ (K_{II} + K)$

Defining $(1 - t_I) = (1 - t_I^*)/(1 - s_I)$, then t_I (the relative tax rates placed on domestic and foreign income in country I) becomes the tax policy parameter for country I and (1) becomes

(2) $(1 - t_I) \ f_I'(K_I - K) = (1 - t_{II}) \ f_{II}'(K_{II} + K)$

For country I (the lending country), the problem is to set t_I so as to obtain the maximum value of total income (that originating domestically and also that received from abroad). More formally, the problem is to maximise (3).

(3) $f_I(K_I - K) + (1 - t_{II}) \ f_{II}'(K_{II} + K) \ K$

subject to (2).
From this one obtains

(4) $f_I'(K_I - K) = (1 - t_{II}) \ (f_{II}'(K_{II} + K) + Kf_{II}''(K_{II} + K))$.

Substituting (4) into (2) gives the solution

(5) $t_I = \dfrac{Kf_{II}'' \ (K_{II} + K)}{f_{II}'(K_{II} + K) + Kf_{II}''(R_{II} + K)}$

If $t_{II} = 0$ (4) gives

(6) $f_I'(K_I - K) = f_{II}'(K_{II} + K) + Kf_{II}'' \ (K_{II} + K)$

i.e. country I chooses a tax parameter (given by (5)) so as to equate the marginal product of capital employed domestically to the marginal revenue derived in country II by lending abroad.
For country II the problem is to maximise (7)

(7) $f_{II}(K_{II} + K) - (1 - t_{II}) \ f_{II}'(K_{II} + K) \ K$

subject to (2).
This gives

(8) $f_{II}'(K_{II} + K) = (1 - t_I) \ (f_I'(K_I - K) - Kf_I'' \ (K_I - K))$

and using (2) gives

(9) $t_{II} = \dfrac{Kf_I''(K_I - K)}{f_I'(K_I - K) - Kf_I''(K_I - K)}$

If $t_I = 0$, (8) gives

$t_{II}'(K_{II} + K) = f_I'(K_I - K) - Kf_I''(K_I - K)$

i.e. country II chooses a tax parameter (given by (9)) so as to equate the marginal product of capital employed domestically to the marginal cost of borrowing abroad from country I.

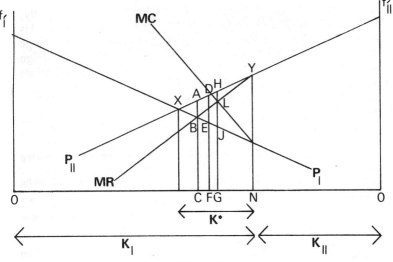

Figure 2

In the absence of any tax in country II, country I will attempt to secure a capital flow NC through a tax AB/AC; whereas in the absence of any tax in country I, country II will attempt to secure a capital flow NF through a tax DE/DF. In fact both countries will finish up taxing income from capital (such as at a situation G) which from a world point of view does not produce as much output as the capital flow K*.

Hamada's model thus illustrates the incentives countries have to tax both investment income being paid abroad and that being received from abroad differently from capital income originating domestically even though in practice these incentives are more complex than in this simple model and extend beyond questions of tax rate policy.

B Tax havens

The preceding discussion has emphasised the incentives for tax authorities to respond to the actions of other tax authorities in connection with the international tax treatment of multinational enterprises. These incentives are clearly reflected in the existence of tax havens, a feature of some potential importance for multinational enterprises. Tax havens are typically very small communities with independent tax authorities who have come to realise that by charging little or no tax on transactions within their jurisdiction, a potential is created for substantial financial flows through their country with beneficial effects. Each transaction tends to receive preferential tax treatment relative to a major industrialised economy. One might think that the citizens of a haven could gain even more by pursuing a tax policy similar (and only slightly more advantageous) to that adopted in large countries. As there are a number of such havens there is typically a substantial responsiveness of financial flows through any particular haven with respect to even a small change in tax rates and so little change from a very preferential tax treatment within each haven tends to occur. Of course, it is not sufficient that a favourable tax treatment alone exists, a stable political and social climate[4] is also necessary. In some cases favourable[5] double tax arrangements with the larger countries with which multinational enterprises deal can be advantageous; in other cases it has been suggested that the lack of double taxation agreements is an attraction as the absence of agreements to exchange information preserves the anonymity of tax haven operations.

A legal tax advantage which tax havens can accord to multinational enterprises is an advantage of delay in paying tax (previously referred to as the deferral privilege). Funds which come into a tax haven can remain there tax free (or at very low rates of tax on income generated on the profits) until such time as they are repatriated to a parent company. In periods of substantial inflation and high interest rates such a deferral privilege can mean an effective exemption from taxation if the company involved is able to earn enough income in the interim to meet its tax liability. It should be emphasised, however, that this advantage accrues predominantly in those cases of subsidiaries of parent companies located in countries operating a credit system of double taxation relief (such as the UK and the US) rather than an exemption system. In the case of the UK exchange control regulations operated by the Bank of England do require some information be given before the establishment of a tax haven operation; in the US this is not so and concern has been

---

12.4 Examples such as the Cayman Isles, New Hebrides and the Bahamas would satisfy this criterion. It is interesting to note that a recent general election in Grenada involved discussion of ways in which to make Grenada into a tax haven. This discussion could, itself, be taken as further commitment to a stable tax haven policy.

12.5 The Netherlands Antilles is a notable example, having treaties with Holland. It has been argued that this provides a cheap route (from a tax viewpoint) in and out of the tax haven area from Western Europe as withholding taxes (which are much higher where treaties do not exist) are reduced by treaty with Holland.

expressed by some writers on this point (see **P.B.** Musgrave, op. cit.) although controls of a different nature do exist.[6]

Tax havens represent an area where it is difficult to assess accurately the conflicting claims that are often heard as to their importance; and it is to be emphasised most strongly that knowledge of the precise role and extent of tax haven activity as it relates to multinational activity is very limited. Tax havens are designed to be attractive not just to large companies but also to persons, trusts, and, one suspects, the fraudulent. Different areas are tax havens for different major economies (the Caribbean and the Channel Islands for the UK; Lichtenstein, Switzerland and Luxembourg for West Germany, the New Hebrides for Australia; Panama, among others, for the US; the Netherlands Antilles for Holland, and so on). It would seem that besides low taxes, one of the features which some tax havens have to offer is anonymity and as already mentioned certain tax havens frequently publicise the fact that they do not have double taxation treaties with the major economies and so no exchange of information is possible between authorities in the tax haven and elsewhere. This could be of considerable importance in constructing a maze of complications which may defeat tax authorities; indeed it is not unknown for a transaction which is basically domestic to an economy to be conducted through a tax haven intermediary (even though no money may go to the tax haven) with the intent, presumably, of frustrating domestic tax authorities. How much of this activity takes place and the extent to which it involves the major multinational enterprises is unknown. Our impression is that much tax haven activity is more concerned with persons, trusts and small companies rather than with the larger multinational undertakings,[7] but firm empirical support for such a claim is difficult to obtain.[8]

12.6 See the discussion of the US position in L.B. Krause and K.W. Dam *Federal Tax Treatment of Foreign Income* Brookings Institution, 1964. The sections of the Revenue Act of 1962 designed to nullify tax haven operations contained important exemptions such as the exemption of shipping companies, with the result that US oil companies by and large conduct shipping operations through Liberia which is reputed to have the largest registered merchant shipping fleet in terms of tonnage of any nation in the world.
12.7 A recently published book by Chown (J.F. Chown *Taxation and the Multinational Enterprise*) provides some information on tax haven operations. Discussing the Bahamas, Chown (p. 123) states 'The Bahamas are perhaps the best known and most widely used of the tax havens. In 1969, for instance, no fewer than 3,200 companies were incorporated, although after that there was a sharp fall in the rate of incorporation. There are now (February 1973) well over 12,000 companies incorporated in the Bahamas of which about one half are connected with finance or financial services. Many of these are, of course, mere brass plate operations. There is a substantial body of genuine and active banks,

Nonetheless, tax havens illustrate the more general problem of governments in one tax jurisdiction responding to the actions of other governments elsewhere. This problem of national interest is as we have stated previously one of the pervasive themes of the difficulty of justifying or designing particular tax treatments of multinational enterprise. In the next chapter we try to examine some recent proposals for approaching this problem via international co-operation in the context of proposals for unified corporate taxation arrangements to operate within the EEC.

---

trust companies and other financial organisations, even after the excellent initiatives taken by the Bahamanian Monetary Authority to eliminate and expel the disreputable fringe.' Chown's figure of 12,000 companies incorporated in the Bahamas should be contrasted with the figure of 11,000 registered paid up companies in the UK in 1966 and 400,000 private companies in the same year. These UK figures are quoted in *National Accounts Statistics: Sources and Methods* ed. Rita Maurice, HMSO 1967 p. 202. The interested reader is also referred to Chown's discussion of the Lichtenstein *Anstalt* (p. 137). Even from information such as this, however, it is not possible to tell what refers to activity of multinational enterprises, and what refers to smaller independent company operations.

12.8 Indeed it can be claimed that not only is it not unknown for multinational enterprises to establish subsidiary holding companies in tax havens, but that surveys in business magazines such as *Fortune* have shown that most multinational operations do, in fact, have at least one subsidiary in a tax haven (some, of course, will have several such subsidiaries in tax havens). It is also fair to say that while a high proportion of tax haven activity in the sense of companies and trusts established, and even more, in the sense of services provided by banks, lawyers and advisers in tax havens, may relate to individuals and small companies, the comparatively few transactions put through tax havens by multinational enterprises may be so large as to account for the majority of the financial volume involved.

13. Proposals for the harmonisation of corporate tax systems in the EEC

In August 1975 the EEC Commission submitted to the Council of Ministers proposals for harmonisation of corporate tax systems within the EEC together with a draft directive.[1] In this chapter these proposals will be discussed and some examples given of the way in which they would operate. It should be noted at the outset that these proposals do not apply to investment funds or unit trusts.[2]

A Outline of the proposals

The Commission recommends a common imputation system and a common system of withholding taxes.[3] The Council has not recommended a common rate of corporation tax and tax credit, but under its proposals the rate of corporation tax and the tax credit must be within a permitted range.[4] The rate of corporation tax must be between 45% and 55%[5] and the tax credit must be not lower than 45% and not higher than 55% of the corporation tax which would be charged on the dividend grossed-up by reference to that corporation tax.[6]

13.1 'Proposal for a Council Directive concerning the harmonisation of systems of company taxation and of withholding taxes on dividends' transmitted to the Council by the Commission on 1 August 1975; hereafter referred to as the draft harmonisation directive.
13.2 See article 2, paragraph 1 of the draft harmonisation directive.
13.3 See ibid. article 1, paragraph 1.
13.4 i.e. the amount of the imputation.
13.5 See article 3 of the draft harmonisation directive.
13.6 i.e. the dividend distributed plus the underlying corporation tax on that dividend.

The Commission proposes a common withholding tax on dividends at the rate of 25%.[7] A credit for that withholding tax will be given in taxing the dividend in the hands of the recipient shareholder whether or not the dividend has crossed a border between member states.[8] In the case of dividends paid by a subsidiary[9] to its parent there will be no withholding tax whether the companies are resident in the same or different member states and the dividend will either be exempt from corporation tax in the hands of the parent or 95% of it will be exempt if the destination country exercises its option to tax 5% of the dividend received from the subsidiary.[10] For the sake of simplicity it will be assumed in the discussion and examples which follow that the member states concerned do not exercise that option to charge 5% of such dividends.

The proposals contain provisions which enable the tax credit granted by the member state of origin to be carried across and set against the recipient shareholder's liability in the destination member state.[11] This will involve the destination member state in granting a credit in respect of tax levied by the member state of origin. There are provisions for financial compensation between the member states concerned[12] whereby the member state of origin must bear the cost of the tax credit which the destination member state has had to give to the shareholders. The broad effect of these provisions is, therefore, that the destination member state's share of the tax on the income flow will be corporation tax on the underlying profit minus the tax credit and the destination member state's share will be tax at the shareholder's marginal rate on the net dividend plus the tax credit, i.e. a form of tax sharing.

The proposals contain a further radical provision, namely that where there is a parent-subsidiary relationship (as defined)[13] the tax credit granted by the member state of origin is carried through to the individual shareholders in the parent company and can be set against their liability to personal income tax in the destination member state.[14] Again there are provisions requiring the member state of origin to pay financial compensation to the destination member state, producing a

---

13.7 See ibid. article 14.
13.8 See article 16, paragraph 1 of the draft harmonisation directive.
13.9 As defined by ibid. article 2, paragraph 1.
13.10 See article 4 of the draft Directive on Parent-Subsidiary Relationships transmitted to the Council by the Commission on 16 January 1969; hereafter referred to as the draft parent-subsidiary directive.
13.11 See ibid. articles 4 and 5.
13.12 See ibid. article 13.
13.13 See note 8 above.
13.14 See the draft Harmonization Directive Articles 9 and 10.

tax-sharing.[15] Thus where a parent-subsidiary relationship exists, at the end of the day only one amount of corporation tax and only one amount of personal income tax on dividends will have been exacted from an inter-corporate income flow which has crossed boundaries between member states, but remained throughout within the perimeter of the EEC. Thus the proposals produce a result within the EEC similar to the UK franked investment income and group income provisions.

B   More detailed consideration

1   Common imputation system

a   Corporation tax. Article 1, paragraph 1 provides
'The member states shall adopt:-
- a common imputation system of corporation tax
- a common system of withholding tax on dividends in accordance with the provisions of the following articles.'
  Article 3, paragraph 1 provides
'Each member state shall apply a single rate of corporation tax to the profits, whether distributed or undistributed, of its corporations. This rate, called the normal rate, may not be lower than 45% nor higher than 55%.'
Article 3, paragraphs 2 and 3 give member states limited power to depart from that permitted range of rates for reasons of economic, regional or social policy.

b   Imputation tax credit. Article 4, paragraph 1 provides
'A dividend distributed by a corporation of a member state shall confer on its recipient a right to a tax credit at the rate referred to in article 8, provided:
a) that he is resident in a member state, and
b) that he is subject to a tax on income or profits in such a way that the full amount of the dividend increased by the tax credit is taken into account in arriving at the amount of his taxable income or profits.'
  Article 8 provides
'1. Each member state shall fix the rate of the tax credit attached to the dividends distributed by the corporations of that state.
2. There shall be only one such rate in each member state. It shall be determined in such a way that the tax credit shall be neither lower than 45% nor higher than 55% of the amount of corporation tax at the normal rate on a sum representing the distributed dividend increased by such tax.'

13.15 See ibid. Article 13, paragraphs 1 and 3.

The permitted tax credit is calculated as a percentage of the dividend grossed-up by reference to the underlying corporation tax charged on it. Some imputation systems (for example the UK) calculate the tax credit as a fraction or percentage of the net dividend. The formula for turning the article 8 percentage into a percentage of net dividend is

$$\frac{X}{100-X} \times Y = Z$$

where X is the percentage rate of corporation tax and Y is the article 8 percentage, and Z is the tax credit expressed as a percentage of the net dividend.

The formula for turning a credit expressed as a percentage of net dividend into an article 8 percentage using the same algebraic functions as above is:

$$Y = \frac{Z \times (100-X)}{X}$$

Thus to discover whether the UK ACT/tax credit is within the permitted band, one must first translate the fraction of 35/65ths into a percentage = 53.85% and then apply the UK rates into the second formula set out above:

$$Y = \frac{53.85 \times (100-52)}{52} = 49.71\%$$

Accordingly the UK ACT/tax credit expressed as a percentage computed in accordance with article 8 is 49.71% which is within the permitted range.

2   Withholding tax

Article 14 provides

'1. Subject to the provisions of the conventions concluded between member states and third countries, each member state shall impose a withholding tax of 25% on the dividends distributed by the corporations of that state, no matter who is the recipient of those dividends.

2. By way of derogation from the provisions of paragraph 1, no member state shall impose a withholding tax on a dividend distributed by a subsidiary to a parent corporation resident in any member state.'

a Dividends paid to a shareholder other than a parent (as defined).[16] Except where a parent-subsidiary relationship exists, dividends, whether crossing the borders of member states or not, will be subject to

---

13.16 See section (b).

a withholding tax at the rate of 25%. Unlike the withholding taxes charged under the usual international arrangements on dividends which cross national boundaries, the withholding tax under article 14 is not designed to ensure that the country of origin is able to charge some tax on the dividend flowing abroad. The purpose of the article 14 withholding tax is simply to combat evasion by shareholders who do not declare in their returns the dividends they have received. The withholding tax levied under article 14 is allowed as a credit against the shareholder's ultimate tax liability, whether he is resident in the member state which exacted the withholding tax or a different member state. The authority for that is article 16 which provides:–

> 'The tax withheld under article 14 shall be set off against the amount of the tax on income or profits to which the recipient of the dividends is liable in respect of them.
> 'The tax withheld shall be repaid to the recipient by the member state which charges the tax on income or profits referred to in the previous subparagraph, to the extent that it exceeds the amount of that tax, or where the recipient has no net liability to tax.'

b Dividends paid by a subsidiary to its parent (as defined). In the case where there is a parent-subsidiary relationship no withholding tax will be levied on the dividend paid by the subsidiary to its parent whether the parent is resident in the same member state as the subsidiary or in a different member state. The reason for this is that the dividend[17] will be exempt from corporation tax in the hands of the parent[18] and therefore no question of evasion arises at that stage. Dividends received by individual shareholders in the parent company will be subject to withholding tax at 25%.

Article 2, paragraph 1, of the draft harmonisation directive incorporates the definition of a parent-subsidiary relationship from the draft parent-subsidiary directive. The latter provides that a parent-subsidiary relationship exists where either
1) one company has a participation of at least 20% in another company or
2) where one company has obtained a participation of any size in another company in exchange for a transfer of assets to that other company. In each case the special privileges accorded to parents and subsidiaries are denied if the qualifying participation does not subsist for at least two years.

13.17 Or 95% of it.
13.18 See p. 134 and p. 138.

In addition it is proposed that any member state shall have the right to treat any of its corporations as parents even though they do not have the requisite 20% participation and if that option is exercised the tax provisions relating to parent-subsidiary relations will apply.

3 Inter-corporate dividends where a parent-subsidiary relationship exists

It is not proposed to deal with the tax treatment of inter-corporate dividends where there is no parent-subsidiary relationship because, first they are particularly complicated and, secondly as a 20% participation constitutes a parent-subsidiary, most multinational enterprises will fall within the parent-subsidiary category.

a   The rules. The rules governing intercorporate dividends where there is a parent-subsidiary relationship are as follows
(i) No withholding tax will be charged on the dividend paid by the subsidiary.[19]
(ii) The dividend[20] will be exempt from corporation tax in the hands of the parent company.[21]
(iii) The parent will be allowed the tax credit given by the member state of origin.[22]
(iv) Under article 9 the parent company will have to charge what is called 'compensatory tax'[23] when it pays a dividend to its shareholders out of the dividend received from the subsidiary.[24]
(v) In cases where there is a parent-subsidiary relationship and the parent redistributes the dividend from the subsidiary within five years of receiving it, the compensatory tax is calculated on the dividend received by the parent plus the tax credit given by the member state where the subsidiary is resident.[25]
(vi) The rate of compensatory tax is such a rate as will produce an amount of compensatory tax equal to the tax credit granted by the

---

13.19 Article 14, paragraph 2 of the draft harmonisation directive.
13.20 Or 95% of it.
13.21 See article 4 of the draft parent-subsidiary directive.
13.22 See articles 4 and 5 of the draft harmonisation directive.
13.23 It would appear that the compensatory tax is levied on the dividend *gross* of the compensatory tax.
13.24 It should be noted that the charge to compensatory tax is not confined to cases where there is parent-subsidiary relation, but, as has been indicated above, it is not proposed to deal with cases where the companies are not parent and subsidiary.
13.25 See ibid. article 10.

member state in which the parent is resident. The provisions dealing with inter-corporate dividends where there is a parent-subsidiary relationship only produce the intended result if the rate of compensatory tax is arrived at by ascertaining what rate it would be necessary to levy on the distribution by the parent plus the imputation tax credit accorded by the member state in which the parent is resident so as to ensure that the amount of compensatory tax is equal to that imputation tax credit.[26] However, it is important to understand that the rule enunciated above is used only for the purpose of calculating the rate of compensatory tax and that the tax base upon which compensatory tax is charged in the case of parent-subsidiary relationships is the net dividend received by the parent from the subsidiary plus the imputation tax credit accorded by the member state in which the subsidiary is resident.[27] The formula for working out the rate of compensatory tax where the tax credit is expressed as a percentage of the dividend net of tax credit is:–

Rate of compensatory tax $= \dfrac{X \times Y}{Z}$

where

X = the dividend net of tax credit, but gross of withholding tax,
Y = the rate of tax credit expressed as a percentage of that net dividend, and
Z = the dividend plus the tax credit.
Thus if the rate of tax credit is 50% of the net dividend[28] the rate of compensatory tax is

$$\frac{50 \times 50}{75} = 33.33\%$$

Therefore, on a net dividend of 50 the tax credit will be 25. Compensatory tax levied on the dividend and tax credit (i.e. $50 + 25 = 75$) at 33.33% would be 25. Thus the terms of article 9 are complied with because the amount of compensatory tax is equal to the tax credit.

In the case of the UK system the tax credit (i.e. ACT) is expressed as a fraction and therefore in order to calculate the rate of compensatory tax it is necessary to translate that fraction into a percentage and then apply the formula set out above. The UK tax credit expressed as a

---

13.26 The commentary on the draft harmonisation directive states that this is the case, (See Bulletin of the European Communities, Supplement 10/75, page 11, footnote 1), but although it is possible to interpret article 9, paragraph 1 in such a way as to produce that result it is submitted that the text should be amended in order to make this abundantly clear.
13.27 See paragraph (v) above.
13.28 As in the case of the French system.

percentage is 35/65 × 100 = 53.85%. The rate of compensatory tax for the purposes of the UK system is:–

$$\frac{65 \times 53.85}{100} = 35\%$$

Article 9, paragraph 3 provides that where the domestic tax code in the state where the parent is resident charges an advance payment of corporation tax at least equal to the tax credit compensatory tax need not be charged; this is because the advance corporation tax performs the function of a compensatory tax. Thus if these proposals are accepted, the UK need not levy any compensatory tax because ACT will perform the same function.

(vii) The tax credit granted by the member state of origin can be set against the compensatory tax chargeable in the destination member state and only the excess of compensatory tax over that tax credit need be paid.[29] Where the destination member state levies an advance corporation tax, the tax credit granted by the member state of origin can be set against the advance corporation tax chargeable in the destination member state and only the excess if any will be payable.[29]

Since the UK ACT is levied on the net dividend paid,[30] and since the net amount of dividend which can be paid will depend upon the amount of ACT payable, the calculation of the ACT liability can be rather complex.[31]

Where both member states have the same tax credit, the origin tax credit will exactly cancel out the destination compensatory tax. If the origin tax credit is smaller than the compensatory tax, the parent company will have to pay the balance to the fiscal authorities in the destination member state. If the origin tax credit is larger than the compensatory tax, consistency requires that the member state of origin should refund the difference to the parent, but because this would involve further financial compensation and administrative problems it is proposed that no refund be made.[32]

(viii) The individual shareholders in the parent company will receive their dividend plus the tax credit at the rate which applies in the destination member state.[33]

The effect of article 10 is that the parent must redistribute the dividend

---

13.29 See ibid. article 10, paragraph 1.
13.30 Unlike compensatory tax which is levied on the dividend paid (gross of compensatory tax) + the origin state tax credit.
13.31 See example 4 below.
13.32 See the commentary in the Bulletin of the European Communities, Supplement 10/75 page 11, paragraph 31.
13.33 See article 4, paragraph 1, article 5, and article 8 para 1.

within five years of receiving it in order to secure the benefit of this favourable system and article 12 contains rules for determining whether the dividend paid by the parent is to be treated as paid out of income carrying an imputation tax credit or out of sources which do not carry such a credit;[34] the general rule is that it shall so far as possible be treated as paid out of the former.

b   Effect of the rules. These rules would have the effect of carrying the tax credit attached to the dividend in the state of origin through to the shareholders in the parent company, and therefore, if they are adopted, they will cure the problem discussed in chapter 7 and avoid overspill[35] in the case of income flows which remain within the perimeter of the EEC.

The broad effect of these rules is that the individual shareholders in the destination member state will receive exactly the same net dividend out of a profit of 100 accruing to the subsidiary as individual shareholders in the member state of origin would receive where the marginal rate of personal income tax of the two categories of shareholders is the same.[36] To that general proposition there is one exception, namely where the tax credit given by the member state of origin is larger than the compensatory tax chargeable in the destination member state. In that case the individual shareholders will receive the same net dividend out of a profit of 100 accruing to the subsidiary as individual shareholders in the destination member state would receive out of a profit of 100 accruing to a company in the *destination* member state.[37] The reason for this is that the proposals do not require a refund to the parent company of the excess of the origin tax credit over the destination compensatory tax.[38]

Thus generally the proposals will achieve neutrality in the sense that the choice of location within the EEC for the parent and the subsidiaries will not affect the amount of tax eligible on the income flow, except in the case where the origin tax credit is larger than the destination compensatory tax. As far as that is concerned the Council has said that a refund of the excess to the parent company 'would entail practical difficulties; for this reason it appears preferable to depart from the principle of non-discrimination and not to make such a payment.'[39]

13.34 e.g. foreign source income from countries outside the EEC.
13.35 See chapter 11.
13.36 See examples 1, 2 and 4 below.
13.37 On the assumption that the two groups of shareholders have the same marginal rate of personal income tax.
13.38 See example 3 below.
13.39 See the citation referred to in note 30 above.

If adopted these new proposals would further the basic premise upon which the EEC is founded, namely the elimination of factors which inhibit free competition between enterprises in member states. The residence of the shareholders may affect the amount of tax exacted on the income flow,[40] but the location of the enterprises will not.

C Examples

This section will be devoted to consideration of examples designed to illustrate the operation of these proposals. In most of the examples fictional member states and rates of tax have been selected; the object of this is to ensure that the examples illustrate the main effects of the proposals as clearly as possible.

In order to obviate encumbering the examples with the application of withholding taxes in the destination member state, it is assumed in all the examples that the destination member state has been able to exercise its right under article 13, paragraph 3, not to impose any withholding tax on dividends paid by corporations resident in its territory.

1 Examples of inter-corporate dividends where there is a parent-subsidiary relationship (as defined)

In the following examples company A is the parent and company B is its subsidiary. The rates of corporation tax, of tax credit and of basic personal income are as stated in the facts. It is postulated in the case of each example that all the individual shareholders are resident in the same member state as the parent and are liable to personal income tax on the dividends at the basic rate, but not at any higher rates.

It is also postulated in each example that a profit of 100 has accrued to the subsidiary and that in the same financial year the subsidiary and the parent have made the maximum distribution to their respective shareholders.

The results will be set out after the facts of each example and before the detailed working to assist those readers who are only interested in the outcome and not the detailed working.

Example 1, showing the position where all the tax rates in each member state are the same
(i) *Facts.* Company A is resident in member state X and company B is resident in member state Y. Both states have the same tax rates, namely:

13.40 Because the rates of personal income tax may vary from one state to another.

Corporation tax = 50%
Tax credit 50% of net dividend
Basic rate of personal income tax = 30%

(ii) *Results*

State Y: Corporation tax = 50 (of which state Y will have to pay 25 to state X
by way of financial compensation)
Withholding tax = Nil

State Y: Corporation tax = Nil[41]
Compensatory tax = Nil
Personal income tax = Nil[42]
State X must refund to shareholders the surplus tax credit[43] of 2.5.

Overall tax burden:
Dividend net of all tax = 52.5
Effective rate of tax on the income flow = 47.5%

(iii) *Detailed working*

State Y tax: Corporation tax at 50% on company B's profit of 100   = 50
Net dividend paid by company B to company A   = 50
State Y tax credit attached to that dividend[44]   = 25
There will be no state Y withholding tax.[45]

State X tax: Net dividend received by company A   = 50
plus state Y tax credit[46]   = 25

_____
75

There will be no state X corporation tax on the dividend in
company A's hands.[47]
Compensatory tax at 33.33%[48] on 75[49]   = 25
less tax credit[50]   = 25

_____
Nil
_____

_____

13.41 Because it is a dividend received from a subsidiary.
13.42 Because this is more than franked by the tax credit carried through from
state Y.
13.43 The personal income tax liability is 30% : 75 (i.e. net dividend of
50 + tax credit of 25) = 22.5 less tax credit of 25 = Nil.
13.44 See article 4, paragraph 1, article 5, and article 8.
13.45 See article 14, paragraph 2.
13.46 Article 4, paragraph 1.
13.47 See article 4 of the draft parent-subsidiary directive.
13.48 For the calculation of the rate of compensatory tax see above.
Compensatory tax is charged by article 9, paragraph 1.
13.49 The tax credit is included in the tax base upon which the compensatory
tax is charged where a parent-subsidiary relationship exists, see article 10,
paragraph 1.
13.50 Article 10, paragraph 1.

Dividend paid to shareholders in company A	= 50
plus the state X tax credit of	25
	75
Personal income tax at 30% on 75	= 22.5
less state X tax credit[51]	= 25
	Nil

State X must refund the excess credit[52] of 2.5.
State Y must pay to state X the amount of the state Y tax credit i.e. 25.[53]

Dividend in the hands of the individual shareholders of company A net of all tax   = 52.5.

This is the same as the dividend net of all tax on a profit of 100 accruing to a domestic state Y company and distributed to domestic state Y shareholders. That calculation is as follows:

Profit	100
State Y corporation tax	50
	50
Plus tax credit	25
	75
Personal income tax at 30% on 75	= 22.5
Against which the tax credit is set giving a refund of	2.5

Dividend of 50 + refund of 2.5 = 52.5.

In example 1 the reasoning was set out *in extenso* because it was the first example; in the ensuing examples the working will be more briefly described.

Example 2, showing the position where the tax credit in the destination member state is higher than the tax credit in the member state of origin
(i) Facts: Company A is resident in member state X and company B is resident in member state Y.

Tax rates:	State X	State Y
Corporation tax	50%	50%
Tax credit expressed as a percentage of net dividend	55%	50%
Basic rate of personal income tax	30%	30%

(ii) Results:

State Y: Corporation tax	= 50
Withholding tax	= Nil

13.51 See article 4, paragraph 1.
13.52 See article 5.
13.53 See article 13.

State X:	Corporation tax	= Nil
	Compensatory tax	= 1.61
	Personal income tax	= Nil
	Refund of surplus tax credit	= 4.11

Overall tax burden:

Dividend net of all tax = 52.5

Effective rate of tax on the income flow = 47.5%

(iii) *Detailed working*[54]:

State Y tax:	Corporation tax at 50% on company B's profit of 100	= 50
	Net dividend paid by company B to company A	= 50
	State Y tax credit attached to that dividend	= 25
	There will be no state Y withholding tax.	
State X tax:	Net dividend received by company A	= 50
	plus state Y tax credit	= 25
		75
	State X corporation tax on the dividend	= Nil
	Compensatory tax at 35.48%[55] on 75	= 26.61
	Less state Y tax credit	= 25
	Compensatory tax payable	= 1.61

Dividend paid to shareholders in company A is the 50 (received from company B) minus 1.61 compensatory tax   = 48.39

Plus state X tax credit of 55% of 48.39   = 26.61

		75.
	Personal income tax at 30% on 75	22.5
	Less state X tax credit	26.61
		Nil

State X must refund the excess credit of 4.11.

State Y must pay to state X the state Y tax credit of 25.

Dividend in the hands of the individual shareholders of company A net of all tax is the amount paid, 48.39 + refund of tax credit 4.11 = 52.5

Again this is the same dividend net of all tax as would be received by a state Y shareholder in a purely domestic case.

Example 3, showing the position where the tax credit in the destination member state is lower than the tax credit in member state of origin

(i) *Facts:* Company A is resident in member state X and company B is resident in member state Y

13.54 For the relevant citations from the draft directives see the notes to example 1.

13.55 For the formula to calculate this rate see p. 139 above.

Tax rates:	State X	State Y
Corporation tax	50%	50%
Tax credit expressed as a percentage of net dividend	50%	55%
Basic rate of personal income tax	30%	30%

(ii) *Results*:

State Y: Corporation tax	= 50
Withholding tax	= Nil
State X: Corporation tax	= Nil
Compensatory tax	= Nil
Personal income tax	= Nil
Refund of surplus tax credit	= 2.5

Overall tax burden:

Dividend net of all tax	= 52.5
Effective rate of tax on the income flow	= 47.5%

(iii) *Detailed working*:[56]

State Y tax:	Corporation tax at 50% on company B's profit of 100	= 50
	Net dividend paid by company B to company A	= 50
	State Y tax credit attached to that dividend at the rate of 55% on 50	= 27.5
		77.5

There will be no state Y withholding tax.

State X tax:	Net dividend received by company A	= 50
	Plus state Y tax credit	= 27.5
		77.5

State X corporation tax on that dividend	= Nil
Compensatory tax at 33.33% on 77.5	= 25.83
Less state Y tax credit[57]	= 27.5
Compensatory tax payable	Nil

Dividend paid by company A to its shareholders	= 50
Plus state X tax credit of 50% on 50	= 25
	75
Personal income tax at 30% on 75	= 22.5
state X tax credit	= 25
	Nil

State X must refund the excess credit of 2.5

State Y must pay state X the state Y tax credit of 27.5

13.56 For the relevant citations from the draft directives see the notes to example 1.

13.57 N.B. The excess state Y credit is not refunded to company A.

Dividend in the hands of the individual shareholders of company
A net of all tax is 50 + refund of 2.5   = 52.5
This compares with a dividend net of all tax in the hands of
shareholders in a purely domestic state Y case of 54.25[58] and in a
purely domestic state X case of 52.5

*Example 4, showing how these proposals would operate on an income
flow between France and the UK*
(i) *Facts*: Company A is resident in the UK and company B is resident
in France.

Tax rates:	UK	France
Corporation tax	52%	50%
Tax credit expressed as a percentage of net dividend	53.85%[59]	50%

(ii) *Results*:
The answers to this example are tentative because the inter-relation
between the UK ACT and the rules in the directive is unclear.[60]

French tax	Corporation tax	= 50%
	Withholding tax	= Nil
UK tax	Corporation tax	= Nil
	Compensatory tax	= None
	Net ACT liability	= 1.25
	Personal income tax	= Nil

Overall tax burden
Dividend net of all tax   = 48.75
Effective rate on the income flow   = 51.25%

(iii) *Detailed working*
French tax
Corporation tax at 50% on company B's profit
of 100   = 50

13.58 Computed as follows –
   Corporation tax at 50% on a profit of 100 = 50

Net dividend	= 50
Tax credit is 55% of 50	= 27.5
	77.5
Tax at 30% on 77.5	= 23.25
Less tax credit of	27.50
	Nil

   Refund = 4.25 + 50 (dividend) = 54.25
13.59 The U.K. tax credit is 35/65ths of the net dividend $\frac{35}{65} \times 100 = 53.85\%$.
13.60 See footnote 30.

Net dividend paid by company B to company A   = 50
plus French tax credit   = 25

                                              ———
                                              75

There will be no French withholding tax.

UK tax

Before computing the UK liability it is necessary to set out the method of computing the ACT on such dividends. ACT under the UK system is charged on the dividend net of ACT. Article 10, paragraph 1 allows the origin tax credit[61] as a credit against the ACT. This congeries of propositions produces the result that the amount of ACT payable depends upon the amount of the net dividend and the amount of the origin credit; in turn the amount of the net dividend depends upon the amount available for distribution and the amount of ACT payable. It is submitted that ACT is chargeable on such an amount as will after payment of ACT minus the origin tax credit equal the amount available for distribution. Expressed algebraically that is:–

$$\text{Net dividend} = \frac{100(a + b)^{62}}{10 + c}$$

where a = Gross sum available for distribution
      b = Amount of tax credit granted by the member state of origin attributable to a
      c = UK rate of ACT expressed as a percentage.

Net dividend received by company A   = 50
                                   Plus French tax credit   = 25

                                                                ———
                                                                75

UK corporation tax = Nil
UK net dividend where 50 is available for distribution =

$$\frac{100\ (50 + 25)}{100 + 53.85} = 48.75$$

ACT of 35/65th on 48.75   = 26.25
    Less French tax credit   = 25

                                                            ———
    Net ACT liability   = 1.25
                                                            ———

————————————

13.61 i.e. here the French tax credit.

13.62 Or, expressing ACT as a fraction, net dividend = $\dfrac{65\ (a + b)}{100}$

Dividend paid to shareholders in company A is the 50 (received from company
B) minus 1.25 ACT   = 48.75
                                                            Plus UK tax credit   = 26.25

                                                                                                     75
UK basic rate personal income tax at 35% on 75   = 26.25
                                                            Less UK tax credit   = 26.25

                                                                                                    Nil

France must pay to the UK the French tax credit of 25.
Dividend in the hands of the individual shareholders of company A net of all
tax   = 48.75
This is the same as the dividend net of all tax which would be received in a
purely domestic case by a French shareholder whose marginal rate was 35%.

        Profit   = 100
        French corporation tax   = 50

                                                    Net dividend   = 50
                                                    French tax credit   = 25

                                                                                75
                                    75 at 35%   = 26.25
        Less French tax credit   = 25.00

                                    Net liability   = 1.25
Dividend net of all tax 50 − 1.25   = 48.75

2   An example of direct foreign investment

The following example illustrates the treatment under these proposals
of a dividend received by an individual resident in one member state in
respect of his shareholding in a company resident in another member
state.

Example 5. X is an individual resident in the UK and he owns all the
shares in company Y which is resident in France. X is liable to tax in the
UK at only the basic rate.

French tax
Corporation tax at 50% on a profit of 100 accruing to
company Y   = 50
Company Y decides to distribute the remaining 50 to X
        Dividend   = 50
        French tax credit   = 25

                                                                                75

France will withhold tax at 25%.[63]
    Withholding tax at 25% on 50[64]   = 12.5
UK tax
X will receive 37.5.
That amount grossed up by reference to the French withholding tax
                                                                     = 50
and the French tax credit must be added   = 25

                                                                   ―――
                                                                      75
UK income tax at 35% on 75   = 26.25
    Less French tax credit of   25
    Less French withholding tax of   12.5   37.5
The UK must refund the excess.
                                      37.5 minus 26.25[65]   =   11.25

            Amount received   = 37.5 (net dividend)
                                 + 11.25 (refund)
                                 ―――――――
            Dividend net of all tax   48.75
                                       ―――――

This figure of 48.75 is the same as the net dividend which a French
shareholder whose marginal rate was 35% would receive in a purely
domestic French case.
    France must pay to the UK the French tax credit of 25[66] plus the
withholding tax of 12.5.[67]

D Summary

The authors are of the opinion that the proposals explained above
dealing with dividend flows between parents and subsidiaries (as
defined) represent an advance from current arrangements in the EEC.
By introducing a kind of international franked investment income
system they will ensure that such income flows are subjected to only one
charge to corporation tax and only one charge to tax on dividends.

―――――――――――――――

13.63 Ibid article 14, paragraph 1.
13.64 It seems that the withholding tax will be charged on the dividend
exclusive of the tax credit.
13.65 The refund of French tax credit is required by article 5 and the refund of
French withholding tax is required by article 16, paragraph 1.
13.66 Article 13, paragraph 1.
13.67 Article 17, paragraph 1.

In essence the proposals are a tax sharing system. The income from the subsidiary is subjected to the corporation tax system of the source country and then the tax levied is shared between the source country and the destination country by means of inter-state financial compensation. The overspill problem would be obviated in the case of dividend flows between parents and subsidiaries (as defined) within the EEC, because the dividend flow would be exempted from corporation tax in the destination country and the tax credit would be carried across to the shareholders in the parent company. The compensatory tax coupled with the provisions for compensation between states would relieve the destination country of the disagreeable phenomenon of having to refund to poor or exempt shareholders tax which it had not collected.

There are, however, a number of aspects of these proposals which may arouse opposition from various member states. First they depend upon the adoption of a common imputation system which will be unpalatable (if not unacceptable) to those member states who are wedded to the classical system (notably Holland).[68] Secondly, the requirement that the member state of origin must bear the budgetary cost of the tax credit given to foreign shareholders by paying financial compensation to the destination member state may arouse the opposition of member states which are net exporters of dividend income within the EEC because they will have to give up part of the tax which they receive under the present system. Thirdly, the introduction of neutrality within the EEC may not commend itself to those member states which are a more attractive location as a result of the existing differing regimes.

For example, at present the Dutch participation exemption coupled with low rates of withholding tax make Holland an attractive situs for such companies. If such harmonisation proposals are adopted, dividends will flow between subsidiary and parent companies based within the EEC without withholding tax and without any corporate tax in the destination country. This will have the effect of making all other member states as attractive as Holland as a situs for holding companies whose subsidiaries are located in other member states. Holland will remain a more attractive situs where dividends are passing from non-EEC countries through Holland to other non-EEC countries. Holland therefore has something to lose if these proposals are accepted.

13.68 It should be noted that the English Labour Party introduced a classical system in the UK in 1965 and expressed opposition to the Conservative Government's introduction of the imputation system in 1972; in spite of some comments while in opposition, the Labour Party has not reverted to the classical system even though it is now in office again.

The UK is unlikely to be enamoured of a system which involves the carry through of the origin country tax credit to the UK shareholders in the parent, leaving the UK Revenue to sort out the financial compensation with the origin member state. Also the proposals involve the abandonment within the EEC of the credit system of double taxation relief to which the UK Revenue is so firmly wedded.

The authors have heard it suggested that in order to make these proposals acceptable to member states with socialist governments, it may be necessary to agree to a high common withholding tax to combat evasion and vigorous anti-avoidance measures directed against the use of tax havens.

The authors' view is that the proposed harmonisation system is desirable because it promotes neutrality between tax locations and provides an equitable system for relieving international double taxation within the Community. It is to be hoped that national political interest will not block its adoption.

14. Economic impact of international taxation on multinational enterprises

Introduction

While it is possible to document the legal tax treatment of multinational enterprises, it is much more difficult to assess the economic impact of these arrangements. The type of questions raised in this connection may be listed as follows. How tax conscious are multinational enterprises? To what extent do they have the ability (and to what extent is it exercised) to shift tax liabilities forward or backward? Can multinational enterprises artificially manipulate profits between countries for tax purposes and if so what is the extent of this ability? To what extent is the tax position of multinational enterprises on paper different from the situation as it stands in practice? These are the issues on which we try to make some assessment here and in a following chapter devoted specifically to the so-called issue of transfer pricing.

A   Are multinational enterprises tax conscious?

Although the evidence is somewhat superficial it seems reasonable to suppose that all companies, both domestic and those involved in multinational activity, are substantially aware[1] of the tax implications of

---

14.1 See, for instance, the analysis by Hall and Jorgensen (R.E. Hall and D.W. Jorgensen 'Tax Policy and Investment Behaviour' *American Economic Review*, June 1967) of depreciation provisions in the US corporate tax code where they find substantial impact of changes in accelerated depreciation provisions on investment behaviour. See also Michael G. Duerr 'Tax Allocations and International Business', *Conference Board*, New York 1972, for a discussion of the attitude of multinational enterprise to taxation arrangements.

all actions they take. To argue that companies are indifferent between gross of tax and net of tax rates of return on employed capital when corporation tax rates are often in the region of 50% seems implausible. It is, however, sometimes argued that companies are not tax conscious in the sense that their decisions are not altered too much by changes in tax systems and rates. If by this is meant that tax considerations do not weigh heavily *ex ante* in corporate decisions, then this could also mean that the actual tax differentials involved with various courses of actions (for instance, location in one country rather than another for a subsidiary of a multinational parent company) are rather small. This of course is very different from saying that corporate decisions would remain largely unaltered in the absence of taxation.

Alternatively, it may be that taxes are relatively unimportant to companies in the sense that any company's marginal decisions are unaltered by tax changes. This would be true, for instance, if effective marginal tax rates were largely unaltered by changes in the legal tax code.[2]

One can also hypothesise that the uncertainties of government tax changes allied to the potential ability of multinational enterprises to shift taxes on to consumers, and to 'transfer price' profits into low tax areas can lead multinational enterprises to place less importance on taxation considerations in making their locational decisions than one might expect from an examination of the tax position. One can indeed conceive of multinational enterprises making plans (such as with regard to the location of a manufacturing plant) on the basis of pre-tax profitability on the grounds that rapid and often unpredictable changes in tax laws give a calculation of after tax profits a false sense of precision. Such a strategy would involve relying[3] on a multinational enterprise being able to use inter-group financing and transfer pricing policies (including the use of holding companies in low tax jurisdictions) to record profits where effective tax rates are lowest,[4] and,

---

14.2 This view of corporate taxes as lump sum taxes on companies has been offered, for instance, by Stiglitz (op. cit.).

14.3 For an elaboration of this kind of strategy see T. Horst 'The Theory of the Multinational Firm: Optimal Behaviour under different tariff and tax rates' *Journal of Political Economy*, 1973.

14.4 It should perhaps be emphasised that documentation of the increasingly complex nominal rates of tax that companies might expect to incur through operation in various geographical locations is inevitably incomplete and always to some extent out of date. Generalized estimates of effective (as distinct from legal) rates of tax that multinational operations might face can involve an element of guesswork, and this added uncertainty may itself affect the behaviour of multinational operations.

in addition on the ability of the multinational enterprise to shift some of remaining taxes forward on to consumers. One of the difficulties in pursuing such a strategy is the implied ability of multinational enterprises to make use of any set of transfer prices which it may deem appropriate to its purpose. Strict arm's length pricing provisions by origin countries and by destination countries where parent companies export to subsidiary companies may substantially curtail the capability of multinational enterprises in this regard.

What is of relevance, however, in this discussion is that (the somewhat limited) survey data on multinational enterprises reveals that little importance seems to be attached to taxation considerations by multinational enterprises in deciding between various locational alternatives. Forsyth,[5] for instance, in his study of US investment in Scotland finds that none out of the 105 firms in his sample mention taxation considerations as entering in any way the locational decision of the firm. While Forsyth's finding has been partially contradicted by other researchers (Basi[6] for instance) who find some mention made by industrialists of the tax structure, this might well reflect a feature that tax treatments do not differ too much between the countries being considered by the prospective multinational entrant to a country.

A further point is that if the transactions costs of settlement and resettlement are of a significant order of magnitude in the case of multinational enterprises, it may be that a change in tax treatment within any country may be such as to deter new multinational enterprise from settling in the country but not be such as to drive away subsidiary companies already settled.[7]

B   Can multinational enterprises shift their tax liability?

The issue of the shifting of the corporation income tax was discussed in chapter 3 in connection with domestic companies. The same issue also enters into the discussion of the tax treatment of multinational enterprises. In the case of multinational enterprises things are more complicated than for the domestic cases as the number of possible

---

14.5 D.J.C. Forsyth *US Investment in Scotland*, Praeger, 1971.
14.6 R.S. Basi *Determinants of US direct investment in foreign countries* Kent State University Press, 1966.
14.7 However, Swiss legislation introduced in 1962 affecting foreign owned holding companies located in Switzerland did drive many away. Financial companies of this form are clearly more easily affected due to their greater mobility.

shifting mechanisms increases substantially and this makes it difficult even to begin to identify possible effects of taxation policy in this area. In addition, it is important to qualify the interpretation of shifting in an international context.

In chapter 3 where we examined the issue of shifting of corporation tax in a domestic context we mentioned a view expressed by Prest[8] that the more open an economy the more limited will be the ability of domestic firms to shift increases in domestic taxes via short term price rises due to the threat of foreign competition. The existence of multinational enterprises suggests a degree of openness in the economies concerned and discussion of shifting in such contexts may be of limited importance for that reason alone.

A further issue arises as to whether tax increases in one country (say the destination country) on one part of a multinational enterprise can be shifted in some way by price rises in another country (the origin country). This ability will be limited if competitive products exist in the other country as in contrast to the domestic situation other producers in this country will not be affected by the tax increases. The possibility of tax shifting in this way would only appear to arise if a multinational enterprise is in a monopoly position, in which case a monopoly price should remain largely unaffected by tax factors.

It is also worth making the (perhaps obvious) point that as the evidence on shifting is cloudy and contradictory in domestic situations, little of empirical substance can be said in an international context and the degree of shifting in practice remains unknown. This is not to say the possibility of shifting should be ignored for these cases only that we can only offer speculation rather than fact on this issue.

Let us take the case of a subsidiary of a multinational parent company both producing and selling abroad in an origin country. If this country raises the rate of corporation tax on the subsidiary company's profits, then one possible shifting mechanism for the tax is from the subsidiary company on to the consumers in that country. In this case the subsidiary company will raise its output price in the origin country so as to preserve its net of tax profits. If the tax is completely shifted in this way, then consumers in that country will bear the burden of any tax increase on subsidiary companies operating within their borders and there will be little incentive for the origin country government to increase tax rates on such undertakings.

There are, however, complications which follow from the international aspects of this situation. Suppose the destination country

---

14.8 A.R. Prest *Public Finance* (5th Edition, 1975) p. 362.

operates an exemption system of double taxation relief. Then, the increase in tax in the origin country will not affect the tax position in the destination country on dividends remitted to the parent country. If, however, the destination country operates a credit system of double taxation relief (as in the UK), then the increase in taxes on the subsidiary company in the origin country will give an offsetting credit to the parent company in the destination country.[9]

Thus, with complete forward shifting of corporate taxes in both origin and destination countries and a credit system of double taxation relief in the destination country, an increase in tax rates in the destination country may give an overall result of a shifting of tax liability from the stockholders of the parent company in the country of destination on to the consumers in the origin country. This would correspond to a multinational parent company responding to a tax increase in the destination country by instructing its subsidiary company to raise prices in the origin country.

With no shifting of the tax in either country and a credit system of double taxation relief in the destination country a tax increase in the origin country results in a redistribution of tax receipts between tax authorities. The subsidiary company operating in the origin country is unable to shift the tax forward onto consumers, the consumers in the origin country bear no further tax in the absence of shifting and there is no increase in total tax liability assuming sufficient credit exists in the destination country to cover the tax increase in the origin country.

The issue of shifting becomes even more confused for cases of multinational enterprises which manufacture components or finished items abroad for export either back to a parent company or to a third country rather than for sale in the origin country. In this case, with shifting in the country of sale (i.e. the ability to raise prices in the third country or destination country), any increase in the origin country tax would be shifted on to consumers in countries other than those of the origin country. With no shifting of the tax in this way and in the event of an exemption system operating in the destination country, the shareholders of the parent company would bear the burden of a tax increase by the origin country; with a credit system operating in the destination country the tax authorities in the destination country would bear the burden of the tax increase. Whichever way the shifting argument goes, in this particular case the residents of the origin country

---

14.9 This and following propositions could be further complicated by having rates of tax in the two countries which gave rise to unused tax credits in the destination country.

will not bear the burden of the tax, and there is little incentive to prevent the tax authorities increasing tax rates on multinational undertakings of this form up to the point where the enterprise is indifferent between remaining or leaving.

Whether or not, and to what extent, shifting of corporate taxes by multinational enterprises occurs is of considerable importance to governments in origin countries in designing tax policy towards multinational enterprises. In the absence of shifting, origin country governments can effectively capture the tax proceeds from the destination country government without increasing the burden of the tax on domestic consumers. Countries which are on average net payers of dividends abroad (rather than recipients) seem to have higher corporation tax rates (particularly in less developed economies)[10] and may well reflect this feature.[11]

C Does taxation of multinational enterprises affect factor substitution and economic efficiency?

In assessing the impact of taxation of companies in a domestic setting it was suggested in chapter 3 that an alternative view to the simple notion of shifting of taxation is to cast the issue of company taxation into a more general framework. It was suggested that one could treat company taxation as forming part of a whole system of taxation of income accruing to capital. Taxes on capital income can be treated as being levied at different effective rates of tax on each industry in which case the system of taxation of income to capital introduces a series of distortions which cause an economy to operate at a position which is not 'pareto-efficient'[12] from the point of view of resource use.

A similar approach can be adopted with regard to the international tax treatment of multinational enterprises. In addition to the efficiency losses and the impact on factor substitution from the point of view of

---

14.10 This statement should be qualified somewhat by reference to tax holidays which may be given in countries which have high rates of corporation tax.

14.11 Equally, less developed countries are unwilling to negotiate double tax treaties mutually to reduce dividend withholding tax rates when the income flows are all in one direction. This is reflected in the almost total absence of double taxation treaties between the United States and underdeveloped countries.

14.12 See chapter 3.

each domestic economy, similar features will apply to the world-wide economy. Thus a country which through its system of double taxation relief and/or double taxation treaties causes multinational parent companies to pay higher effective tax rates on capital income than comparable domestic companies introduces a further distortion into the operation of the world-wide price system beyond those present within each domestic economy. Relative to an efficient world-wide allocation of resources, too little capital would tend to be invested abroad and too much invested at home.

A simple transfer of this analysis to the case of multinational activity is, however, a little misleading for a number of reasons. One reason lies in the treatment of the tax revenue in such an analysis. In the case of domestic taxation, tax revenue accrues to the domestic government and may be retained to finance public expenditures or distributed among domestic residents. In the case of taxation of multinational activity, tax revenue is collected on subsidiary company profits in the origin country and no direct[13] benefit from such revenue accrues to the residents of the destination country. A situation where the government in the destination country arranges for the total tax rates on domestic and multinational parent companies to be the same will represent a movement towards an efficient allocation of resources on a world-wide basis but will very likely be an undesirable situation from the viewpoint of the residents of the destination country alone. By taxing multinational parent companies in the destination country so that the total tax rate is higher than that on domestic companies, total world product will be reduced but the destination country may well receive more of the reduced output than it would from the world-wide situation in which there was an efficient allocation of resources. Thus in an international context forces are present which will cause tax rates to be set in such a way as to further deviate the international economy from an efficient allocation.

A second problem with this approach lies in the competitive assumption which is involved in the general view of domestic corporate taxation. It would seem to be the case that multinational activity tends to be more heavily concentrated than purely domestic productive activity Lall,[14] for instance, has reported that in a survey of US firms in 1965 7% of US multinationals (18 firms in the survey data reported) accounted for 65% of intra-firm exports from the US. In the UK he reports ratios

---

14.13 Indirectly they may benefit from a development of the infrastructure in the origin country financed by these tax receipts.
14.14 S. Lall 'Transfer Pricing by Multinational Manufacturing Firms' *Oxford Bulletin of Economics and Statistics*, August 1973.

which are even higher (for 1966) with less than 2% of UK multinational firms accounting for 52% of intra-firm exports, while 76% of multinational firms accounted for only 6% of intra-firm exports. Some writers on multinational companies[15] have made the stronger argument that the phenomenon of multinational activity itself is a result of concentration and monopoly power within domestic economies (particularly the US) and that this concentration must inevitably spill over into the international sphere. Concentration of a small number of firms in particular industries is considered to exist in destination countries and each of these firms is assumed to be aware that attempts to expand domestically will be met by anti-trust or anti-monopoly laws. It is suggested that this situation forces monopoly expansion abroad. Whether or not one subscribes to this view of the origin of multinational activity, there can be no doubting the fact of considerable concentration. Thus in the international sphere the competitive assumptions underlying this general view of the impacts of corporation tax can be questioned.

For these reasons the presumption for equal taxation (in total) for multinational enterprises and domestic companies that obtains from efficiency considerations on a world-wide scale will not hold. This is due both to the situation being viewed separately by each of the countries involved, and the fact that the assumptions underlying this analysis would in this context appear to be weak.

14.15 S. Hymer *The International operations of national firms: a study in direct investment* Unpublished Ph.D Thesis, MIT 1960. R. Caves 'International Corporations: the industrial economics of foreign investment' *Economica*, 1971.

15 The transfer pricing problem

We have so far mentioned that the effective tax rate that a multinational enterprise bears in total on its operations may differ from the legal tax rate one would perhaps expect to prevail. A mechanism which, if used, can cause a divergence between legal and effective tax rates is the use of so called transfer pricing. This matter has received much attention in the literature on multinational companies and is as we mentioned earlier the subject of a certain amount of folklore. It is clearly of substantial importance that this issue be raised in our study but it must be made clear at the outset that we have not undertaken an exhaustive study of the extent of such practices and our remarks are made more by way of summary than as a reflection of original research on the topic.

The term 'transfer pricing' refers to the prices which are used as the accounting basis for recording transactions between multinational parent and subsidiary companies or branches. Obvious examples of such traded items are components manufactured in one country (say by the parent) and 'sold' to another company (say the subsidiary) for use in a higher stage of production in another country. The need for a 'transfer price', however, stretches further than physical commodities into such things as royalties, know-how, research and development, and the interest rate paid on loans between parent and subsidiary companies.

In the majority of these cases a 'fair' or 'appropriate' price must be largely indeterminate but the price which is charged has considerable impact for the tax authorities involved. By charging a 'low' price on traded goods sold by a parent to a subsidiary company, the profit accruing to the subsidiary company is higher (and that accruing to the parent company lower) than it would have been if a 'high' or 'intermediate' price had been charged. Clearly where substantial differentials in the rate of corporation tax exist between countries there is a tax incentive to transfer profits to the low tax country by such a mechanism. Even in the absence of corporation tax differentials, transfer pricing may be of benefit in avoiding dividend withholding taxes on funds transferred between subsidiary and parent companies.

These tax incentives are by no means independent of the arrangements for double taxation relief which exist in various countries.[1] Under an exemption system of double tax relief, for instance, there is an incentive to transfer profits out of the country to a low tax area to be returned on an exempt basis. Another case where these double tax arrangements affect the issue is where a parent country operates a credit system rather than an exemption system of double tax relief. In this case, the parent company may have unused foreign tax credits on foreign income and there is an incentive to transfer domestic profits out of the country and return them in order to use the surplus tax credit. Such a case as this last one raised would be unlikely to occur, however, if foreign corporation tax rates were above the domestic tax rates.

As mentioned above, treaty arrangements also enter the picture with respect to dividend withholding taxes. In some cases, transferred profits may not represent much of a saving[2] where the corporation tax position alone is taken into account, but the saving of dividend withholding taxes abroad can be quite substantial (especially in those c ses where double taxation treaties do not exist). Even where OECD model treaties form the basis of double taxation arrangements and withholding tax rates of 15% apply, the saving of this tax alone can be sufficient incentive to indulge in transferring.

It should perhaps also be pointed out at this stage that transfer pricing problems are not limited to multinational enterprises but also involve domestic companies. A domestic company buying components from or selling components to a subsidiary company also faces the problem of determining an appropriate price on the transaction. This situation causes less concern because, save in unusual circumstances, the total tax received by the central authority and the tax liability of the group of companies involved will be unchanged[3] under varying transfer prices.

15.1 Where further complications could arise would be where a destination country I imposes, say, a 50% tax and an origin country II, say, a 30% tax. The parent company has an incentive to shift profits from I to II by selling intermediate products at low prices. In the case of an exemption system in I, these transferred profits could then be returned from II to I. Under a credit system in I the parent may be taxed (upon repatriation of profits from II) for subsidiary profits it receives.

15.2 These would be cases where the corporation tax rates were set at a similar level in the origin and destination countries.

15.3 In the United Kingdom this is no longer the position with respect to companies engaged in exploration for and extraction of North Sea oil as there

A Transfer pricing – arrangements[4]

Given that multinational companies have both opportunity and incentive to indulge in transfer pricing for tax advantage, the next step is to examine those taxation arrangements in various countries which attempt to regulate transfer pricing. The essence of the problem is that tax authorities must attempt to find where a transaction which is internal to a group of companies takes place at an artificially beneficial price and the near impossibility of this task in many cases cannot be over emphasised. To detect and define a case of transfer pricing authorities must determine appropriate prices that transactions should have taken place at but for supposed attempts to use artificial prices to secure tax advantage. This, in turn, requires the tax authorities to enquire into the intentions and activities of the company involved to decide what price it should be charging in its own interest outside of tax considerations.[5]

In practice this involves the tax authorities in an attempt to determine an arm's length price for the transaction under consideration. The term 'arm's length price' is more tightly defined in some country's statutes than others[6] but the broad approach is to establish a price which would

---

are substantial tax incentives to transfer profits out of the North Sea 'ring fence' established by the government. The UK tax authorities have recognised this and have tried to limit transfer pricing by legislation in this area. It remains to be seen how successful this will be.

15.4 A survey of the situation as it exists in a number of countries is presented in the general report by S.S. Surrey and D.R. Tillinghast to the Twenty-fifth Congress of the International Fiscal Association, Washington, DC 1971.

15.5 This fact, the rigid adherence to a tax reference price by the tax authorities, can cause problems not of the companies' making. See the evidence of Mr A. Lord before the UK Parliamentary Committee of Public Accounts (HC 122) 24 January, 1973. Mr Lord reports that nine oil companies accumulated losses of £1500 million over a period of seven years up to 1972. The explanation of this feature is primarily that with corporation tax rates in the Middle East States at around 55% subsidiary companies abroad could sell crude oil to parent companies in the UK at a little over one half the tax reference (i.e. posted) price and still show a small profit, but the tax reference price used in the Middle East has been used for tax purposes as the cost of crude oil to parent companies in the UK. UK parents, in such cases, have had commercial profits but have accumulated the aforementioned losses (and also paid no taxes in the UK) through no deliberate transfer pricing policy of their own. These losses created further problems connected with preventing an offset of these losses against North Sea oil profits.

15.6 For instance, Surrey and Tillinghast (op. cit) state (pI/8) '. . . some countries appear to have only minimal reallocation provisions and also do not seem to make much use for reallocation purposes of the general rules on the determination of income'. They quote Argentina, Mexico and Spain as examples of countries in this category.

prevail between competitive buyers and sellers in a free market with no collusion.

On the face of it this would seem easier in some cases than in others. Where a world market exists in a physically similar commodity to that traded internally between a parent and subsidiary company, the world price could in principle be used. But where commodities are so distinct in physical characteristics that no clear world price exists the tax authorities have rather obvious problems; and where royalties and know-how are involved no world prices can be used. In fact, the tax authorities' insistence on their own interpretation of an arm's length price for the determination of the tax base may produce a transfer pricing problem where in fact none existed. Furthermore as multinational enterprises are highly concentrated, an arm's length price between competitors may be inappropriate as a price which discounts the tax advantage.

There are also additional factors which may affect the transfer price such as the wish to reduce tariffs on components imported by subsidiary companies, expectations of movements of exchange rates on currency markets, and so on. Indeed, one of the complications faced by tax administrators and researchers alike is that multinational enterprises may well indulge in transfer pricing for reasons such as these in addition to any tax advantage; the tax advantage and these other reasons may even conflict as to the direction the transfer should take.

A further complication affecting the whole issue is that things may even work against multinational enterprises; tax authorities may not agree between themselves on what constitutes an arm's length price with the result that companies may finish up paying tax on more than 100% of their profit. This is a complaint that has been voiced to the authors by some enterprises conducting operations in several countries (in some cases between pairs of EEC countries).

B   Transfer Pricing – Evidence

In practice it is difficult to generalise[7] as to how important the transfer pricing problem is or how much tax reduction takes place via this method.[8]

15.7 It seems useful, at this point, to provide the following lengthy quotation from Surrey and Tillinghast (op. cit) (pages I/10, I/11, I/12) 'The United States, Canada, Germany and the United Kingdom, perhaps in that order, seem to have a more active practice of reallocation. In some European countries, a practice exists but apparently to a lesser extent. Countries where the multinational corporations have only more recently become active are still in the early stages

There are pieces of evidence from various economies which can be quoted, although as regards multinational activity in developed economies the overall view still remains somewhat inconclusive. The situation in less developed economies seems to be more clearly open to transfer pricing as tax differentials between origin and destination countries are larger and tax administration is much laxer.

In the USA the statutory definition of an arm's length price is probably more explicit than for most other economies (section 482 of the IRS code). Section 482 prescribes three methods of determining an arm's length price, these methods being applied by the Revenue agent in sequence; these are (i) a comparable uncontrolled price (ii) a resale price (iii) a cost plus mark up price determination. Where none of these methods can be 'reasonably applied' 'some appropriate method . . . other than those described' may be used.

A recent study[9] of over 500 US multinational enterprises found that in

of developing their reallocation policy. But dividing lines and classifications among countries cannot be sharply expressed.

'The frequency of adjustments in actual practice seems quite limited in some countries. Information received by the Israel Reporter from his country's Treasury indicates that in practice most of the problems have not been faced. In Portugal, the reallocation provisions enacted in 1964 are said not to have been invoked by the tax authorities to date. The Swedish Report indicates that there have been few cases where the application of the reallocation provision have been considered. ... The methods of administration, while exhibiting differences, indicate a considerable reliance on solution at the administrative level, largely through negotiation between tax authorites and tax payers. Thus, the British tax authorities have apparently made few formal applications of the reallocation provision. They rather 'sue the threat of a direction (under the reallocation provisions) to good effect'. Companies which carry out transactions with related entities are usually asked to confirm from time to time that the principles of the section (485) are being followed. .... In Germany, the Netherlands, Switzerland and the United Kingdom, and apparently in Canada, conflicts over inter-company pricing between tax officers and companies are more often solved by bilateral negotiations rather than by the administrative use of the unilateral power to fix a price . . . The influence of extraneous rules on the reallocation practice should also be noted, particularly in the case of the United Kingdom. One of the reasons why there have been few formal applications of the statutory reallocation provision is that for certain international transactions a prior authorisation has to be granted by the Treasury or prior consultations have to be held with the Bank of England for exchange control purposes. . .'
15.8 Chown (op. cit) (p. 94) states that 'There is a grey area within which it is impossible to argue that a transfer price is unreasonable. Part of the art may be to know just how far it is safe to push the principle of under and over invoicing without inciting the tax authorities to invoke the powers of adjustment that they all possess. This will require up-to-date local advice.'
15.9 'A study of corporate experience with section 482' W.F. O'Conner and S.M. Russo: Intertax. *The European Tax Review*, 1973/1–2.

this sample (admittedly of allocations involving not only goods, but also the pricing of intangibles, royalties, fees, and service charges, and intercompany loans), that there was an extraordinarily wide variance of interpretations given to section 482. The fourth method was the one most often used by IRS agents (36% from among 145 allocations reported by surveyed firms where pricing of goods was involved). Methods (i), (ii), (iii) were reported as used in respectively 28%, 13% and 23% of cases. Methods mentioned by companies as being used under the fourth method included: comparison with a foreign customs valuation; various formulae for the division of gross or net profit between manufacturing and marketing units of the multinational undertaking; attribution of all foreign operation income to the parent; and an arbitrary price selected by the IRS agent.

O'Connor and Russo conclude that 'while some executives report that section 482 is the most important determinant of their (intercompany) pricing policies, the majority consider other factors more important'. When asked how they (the executives) would describe the IRS methods used in determining an arm's length price in their own cases responses varied from 'cost plus 20%', 'cost plus 150%', to 'strictly a horse trade' and 'arbitrary'. They also note that ... a substantial proportion of the reported allocations involved transactions with affiliates whose tax rates were lower than the US rate. Despite the higher incidence of allocations involving related units that might be considered tax haven corporations, the respondents reported that many allocations involve foreign affiliates whose effective rate of tax is about the same as the US rate'. In these latter cases companies would presumably have less to gain from a taxation viewpoint by making a transfer abroad.[10]

Thus under a system of determining arm's length prices which is, perhaps, the most clearly defined of any country one has a sense of the inapplicability of the arm's length price regulations within quite wide bands. This is compounded by a feeling that even if an allocation is forced upon a company by the tax authority it will be to a considerable extent arbitrary anyway.

Evidence on the position in less developed economies is provided in an important recent study on transfer pricing in Columbia obtained from research carried out by the Planning Office (Planaecion) and by the Import Control Board (INCOMEX) who compared actual prices used

---

15.10 One could, however, argue that as such transfers are made this must clearly be for other than tax reasons. Such reasons may also exist in other cases, of course, if at the same time a tax saving would result.

by multinationals to comparable world market prices. Vaitsos[11] describes this study and others in Latin America at some length and a summary of findings is given in a recent article by Lall[12] who reports: 'Planeacion discovered a weighted average of over-pricing for a wide range of pharmaceutical imports of 155% (for 1968) and INCOMEX of 87% for 1967-70. ... It was also found that some rubber imports had been overpriced by 44%, some chemical imports by 25% and electrical components by 54%. Moreover studies on transfer pricing undertaken in other neighbouring countries, especially Chile, showed that the pattern was similar.' It is important to point out, however, that in many developing countries (especially in Latin America) interest and royalties paid to a foreign parent company are either not deductible as a cost in determining the corporate tax liability of the subsidiary or are only allowed up to some maximum. These features of the domestic tax system may more than offset any advantage obtained through transfer pricing.

The evidence on the extent or importance of transfer pricing cannot be described as firm and by the very nature of the difficulties involved will undoubtedly remain largely anecdotal.[13] There seems to be considerable concern which is openly expressed about the transfer pricing issue in official circles within the European Commission. In the UK concern within official circles tends in our experience to be less openly voiced.[14] It is obviously an issue, however, that will continue to attract substantial attention.

C Parent and subsidiary loans

The discussion of transfer pricing in the preceding two sections of this chapter has raised the possibilities which may exist for multinational enterprises to 'move' profits from high tax jursidictions to low tax

---

15.11 C.V. Vaitsos *Intercountry Income Distribution and Transnational Enterprises* Oxford University Press, 1974.

15.12 'Transfer pricing by multinational manufacturing firms', S.Lall, *Oxford Bulletin of Economics and Statistics,* August 1974.

15.3 Several rules of thumb abound in the folklore such as that it is a practice engaged in more by US based companies than European based companies; pharmaceuticals and precision instruments (including computers) are sometimes mentioned as the industries of higher incidence. Verification of these stories on any scientific basis has, as far as we are aware, not been attempted.

15.14 Recent changes in the 1975 Finance Act do, however, reflect an attempt to extend the legislative powers of the Inland Revenue in the UK to deal with cases of transfer prices.

jurisdictions by manipulation of the prices which are paid on intermediate products which cross a national boundary for use in a higher stage of the production process and which are internal to the multinational operation. An alternative and in many ways simpler mechanism which achieves the same ends involves the financial structure of the relationship between subsidiary and parent companies. Evidence on the extent to which such a mechanism is used is lacking and here we merely illustrate the way in which the discussion of transfer pricing is relevant to transactions other than those in which commodities are involved.

Earlier, in our general discussion in chapter 3 of corporate taxes in a domestic setting, we mentioned the importance of the financial structure of domestic companies. Interest payments made to service the debt of a company are deductible from profits for the purpose of determining corporate tax liability, and the word 'puzzle' has been used by some economists to describe the feature that domestic companies typically indulge in seemingly small amounts of debt financing relative to the tax incentives involved. It was noted earlier that non-tax considerations enter the debt/equity decision for a domestic company, especially the cost to the company of borrowing funds and the risk of bankruptcy and the threat of merger or takeover, and these may act against the tax incentive in these matters.

When we turn to the multinational parent company with a subsidiary company abroad we find these non-tax considerations no longer apply in the same way to the use of debt instruments between parents and subsidiaries. Should a multinational enterprise wish to 'take' all or most of the profits accruing to a subsidiary company though the parent company it can do this by having a heavily loan financed subsidiary company abroad. As always this possibility can become very complex; for instance, if this method of repatriating funds to parent from subsidiary companies is used rather than an intercompany dividend, there will typically be interest withholding taxes in the origin country. If so, the question arises as to whether the payments of withholding tax are treated as payments of underlying tax for double tax purposes in the country of destination. In particular cases debt financing of this form may actually work against the interest of the parent company although one can envisage cases where it will be preferential, particularly if the parent company is in a low tax territory. Alternatively, the parent may borrow from the subsidiary as a way of moving profits to a low tax origin country.

The use of methods which convert intercorporate dividends into capital gains is also potentially a way of remitting profits with tax savings which may be of significance. Retention of profits by the subsidiary company (if in a low tax area) followed by liquidation of the subsidiary for a holding company may give a considerable tax saving to the parent company owing to the taxation of the capital gains on a realisation basis,[15] and the avoidance of dividend withholding taxes.

These other mechanisms beyond the often considered method of transfer pricing on intermediate products may be of some consequence for the artificial movement of profits by multinational enterprises from the jurisdiction of one tax authority to the other, but as with transfer pricing on goods, the evidence on the extent of these operations is unfortunately sparse.

As we have emphasised in other places in this study, we have done no original research work on the issue of transfer pricing and we have only been able to touch briefly on the matter as one of the components of this monograph. We would point out to the reader that it is the view of some that the question of transfer pricing is the most important of all the issues concerned with taxation of multinational enterprise. Those subscribing to such a view would no doubt claim that if it is not possible to administer taxation arrangements as they are intended, it is of limited value to discuss questions of principle which will only affect the position on paper and not necessarily the position in practice. The reader will no doubt sense that while we are aware that this is an emotive issue on which there are claims and counter claims, our feeling is that the problems of definition and perception in this area make a balanced view extremely difficult to ascertain. While we would not deny the potential importance of transfer pricing, we are unconvinced, at least for developed economies, that its use is so extensive as to modify substantially the tax position of multinational business in practice. Equally, we would not (and should not) put this forward as a definitive view on this matter and we would strongly endorse the need for systematic, independent and careful empirical work on this topic.

15.15 Some care is needed here as many European countries tax capital gains in the hands of a company as ordinary profits. In the UK a system of excluding 11/26ths of the capital gains in the hands of a company operates (so that the effective rate of tax is 30%) and this may be an incentive to use liquidation of foreign subsidiaries in the way suggested in the text.

Concluding remarks

In this monograph we have sought to provide an overview of the tax position of multinational enterprises in developed countries and especially the EEC. We have endeavoured to expound the principle features of the present arrangements, taking the tax systems of particular developed countries as examples. We have sought to examine the rationale of those arrangements together with possible alternatives. To repeat what is stressed in the introduction, we do not attempt to provide a detailed guide, but instead we have concentrated on what we consider to be the principle issues and where detail is provided it is by way of illustration.

It is difficult to summarise the content of this study but we would emphasise the following points by way of conclusion:

1 Tax arrangements affecting multinational enterprises are complicated. Different countries have differing domestic corporation tax systems and rates. Bilateral treaties are entered into by pairs of countries and in addition most countries grant unilateral relief from double taxation. Individual countries give different forms of relief for taxes paid in other countries and different treatments are given to various forms of payments passing between parent and subsidiary companies. All this makes generalisation treacherous. Whatever the reasons for this complexity, it also renders the broad general question whether multinational enterprises on average pay more or less tax than comparable domestic enterprises difficult if not impossible to answer. One can point to tax advantages open to multinational enterprises which are not available to purely domestic enterprises, such as transfer-pricing and use of tax havens, but in our view the popular notion that *all* multinational enterprises employ these avoidance devices is not true. There are undoubtedly instances in which any possible advantages are substantially outweighed by disadvantageous features, such as the extra tax burden suffered by some multinational enterprises which are partly

located in the UK,[1] but the opposite notion that *all* multinational enterprises suffer a disadvantageous tax position is equally untrue.

2   Whether or not multinational enterprises are taxed too heavily depends not only upon accurately determining how much tax they do in fact pay, but also upon what is regarded as a proper amount of tax for them to be required to pay. That latter question depends upon what principles are assumed to dictate an appropriate taxation policy towards multinational enterprises. That is an issue to which the maxim *tot homines quot sententiae* applies, but we would emphasise that we do not regard our *sententia* or that of anyone else as being an absolute universal truth.

3   On the issue of transfer pricing we have explained the nature of the problem and considered examples of the measures which some countries have taken to counteract it. We have not, however, attempted to investigate in detail how much transfer pricing occurs in practice. Indeed we would question whether such an investigation is practicable; anyone undertaking empirical work in this area not only needs to have access to information about the inter-corporate dealings of a large number of multinational enterprises (much of which may not be available to the public) but he also needs a large number of expert valuers to enable him to ascertain whether a price charged in each inter-corporate transaction was artificially high or low. Furthermore the question whether a particular price is artificially high or low may be a difficult question of fact upon which different experts in the field concerned may conscientiously reach different conclusions.

4   Double taxation arrangements are affected by the interaction of the national interests of different countries, and the arrangements which are contained in a bilateral treaty reflect a compromise between the competing interests of the two countries who have negotiated the treaty; for example, the treatment under the new UK/US Treaty of dividends paid by UK companies to US shareholders. In our view these issues of national interest are a prime cause of the complexity and diversity of the present arrangements and a prime obstacle to any fundamental change.

In closing we would reiterate our view that the recent proposals for harmonisation of corporate tax sytems within the EEC are a highly commendable attempt to produce a radical improvement and represent welcome, if limited, progress towards reforming the present arrangements through international co-operation.

16.1 See chapter 11 dealing with the overspill problem.

Index